THE EUROPEAN IDEA

Lord Gladwyn

THE EUROPEAN IDEA

FREDERICK A. PRAEGER, *Publishers*
New York . Washington

BOOKS THAT MATTER
Published in the United States of America in 1966
by Frederick A. Praeger, Inc., Publishers
111 Fourth Avenue, New York 3, N. Y.

Printed in Great Britain

Contents

25515

Introduction

THIS book is not a learned essay: it is a political tract. Many excellent and detailed works have been published lately on various aspects of Britain's relationship to the mainland of Europe. To some slight extent I have myself contributed to this national debate. But the experts will not find here any very new or startling arguments for joining or not joining the Common Market. The facts are now known to all who care to study the subject: what is lacking is the will. Why is it lacking? Partly perhaps because the background, the history and indeed the conception itself have not been fully understood, except by those who have the time and energy to read a number of rather specialized works. What I am thus concerned with is in its broadest sense the European Idea, which I believe is still the great, indeed the dominating, political issue today, not only for Britain but for its closest neighbours: I try to describe what this is in terms of the modern world and I draw the only conclusion which can, as it seems to me, be drawn from any such presentation, namely that, if humanly possible, Britain for economic, but chiefly for political reasons, and also for the good of Europe itself, ought to join the Common Market as soon as this is possible. This assumes, it is true, that the Common Market will endure in some form, which seems on the whole to be probable. I try finally to explain what exactly it would imply for us if we did join and how we could then work towards the establishment of the equivalent of a United States of Europe without any damage to our relations with America and the Commonwealth, still less to our national personality and our great traditions.

I hope I have not underestimated the very real difficulties still in the way of Britain doing anything of the sort. The reader will judge. Of course if we are ever to come in there must be negotiations of some kind, but first of all there must be the will to do so – on both sides of the Channel – and this is not yet manifest. I hope too that the various alternatives confronting us have been objectively stated. This is perhaps more difficult for someone who has in many ways the instincts of a pamphleteer. I trust therefore that I shall not offend by any over-statement or by misrepresentation of views sincerely held by good, patriotic people. I would only ask them to consider dispassionately the evidence that I shall produce. Perhaps I should also confess at this point that I have not always been a convinced European (in the sense of acknowledging the necessity of our accepting some supra-national solution) but was gradually converted to this belief after the war, and notably after the constitution of the Coal and Steel Community in 1951, by what seemed to be the actual logic of events.

The book then is chiefly designed to meet the needs of the ordinary intelligent citizen who is inclined to say that he does not understand the European issue and who may feel (how wrongly!) that it has little relation to everyday political problems. In particular I hope that my presentation will appeal to the younger generation not only in Britain but also across the Channel, who are groping after some political ideal or objective transcending ordinary party politics or conventional nationalist feelings. For them I have sought to show how the acceptance of certain disciplines by the countries of the Old World might transform the political scene and lay the foundations for a wider association of the industrialized nations of the West which alone could heal the breach with the Communist or 'Orthodox' East and thus prepare the way for a yet larger Europe and eventually for the World Federation of the future.

When I say Europe, what exactly do I mean? I mean that part

of geographical Europe which was Christianized from the West or formed part of the Roman Empire. Part of this area is now under alien domination; but all must come together if the European Idea is ever to be accomplished in its fullest sense. On the relationship of Russia with Europe I shall expand later. I am however primarily concerned with a separate and distinct civilization that has always had a personality of its own. It has been said that generalizing about history is only pardonable if it is in order to justify a thesis. The scholars must forgive me if I have occasionally forgotten the trees for the wood!

All beginning is difficult. United Europe is no exception to this rule. But out of the welter of discordant noises and mutual recriminations something is slowly emerging, and though it may still be stifled, it seems at least probable, whatever the follies of rulers for whom the past is more real than the future, that it will endure. What is this collectivity now thrusting itself upward in a dead world, this new thing no longer 'powerless to be born'? It is what some indeed call Europe, others Christendom, known in the Middle East as Feranghistan, or the country of the Franks, the ancient home of Western civilization, whose material values, for good or for evil, reluctantly or willingly, are now generally accepted from China to Peru.

During the last seven hundred years or so this small peninsula of Asia has produced an enormous majority of the world's greatest scientists, poets, musicians, painters, playwrights, novelists, engineers, saints, mystics, explorers, doctors, philosophers, lawyers, historians, economists, social workers, political theorists, astronomers, humanists, men who 'followed knowledge like a sinking star beyond the uttermost bounds of human thought.' It has also produced some of the greatest scoundrels and mass murderers known to history. It has known periods of peace when civilization reached its highest points and other periods of appalling savagery when the whole fabric of society seemed about to come apart. In the last five hundred years it has been responsible for nearly all the great primary inventions in the realm of physics from steam to the splitting of the atom.

In political ideas it ranges from the Quakers to the Dictatorship of the Proletariat; in leadership from Hitler to Pope John XXIII; in literature from Racine to Bond. 'Man without law,' said Aristotle, 'is the worst of the beasts.' Europe divided against itself is the most horrible of human communities. The extraordinary, the god-given, intelligence of Western man then assumes a diabolical form. The corruption of the best is the worst. 'How art thou fallen from Heaven, O Lucifer, son of the Morning.'

At the outbreak of the First World War in 1914 the whole world, for several centuries, had been Europe's oyster. The techniques of Western man, the 'magic' of the Europeans had resulted in Empires and in zones of influence from which very few non-European nations were immune. Many thought that this primacy was in the natural order of things. So it might have been had not the diabolical principle asserted itself and the rule of force prevailed. The mystique of Europe was shattered. The hungry sheep looked up and were not fed. Even the gentle religion of Christ was thought to be a mockery when expounded by the warlike Franks. The old religions with their magical and bloody rites re-emerged in many places. New nationalisms parodied the grotesque example of the Metropolis. The Western God had failed.

In 1945, at the end of the third 'Thirty Years War', it certainly looked as if Europe had succeeded in her last attempt at self-destruction. Nobody who, like myself, was in Berlin shortly after the defeat of Hitler, or even one who was in Paris during the terrible winter of 1945 could have thought that Europe was anything but down and out. Twenty years later, thanks to her own efforts, but also largely to extraordinary prescience and political courage on the part of her 'daughter' – America – she now has another and no doubt a final chance. True the suicidal instinct is still in her blood. It is popularly known as national-ism, and though owing to circumstances which have never before prevailed, it may this time be held in check, this is not certain even if with every year that passes it becomes more likely.

So will this dream of European unity, including the reunion of the Germans within a larger whole, now at last be fulfilled? Or will it once again be destroyed by the 'practical politicians', the 'infallible guides', who occasionally identify themselves with the nation-state, or just the paranoiac demagogue? Nobody can say. This time – the last time – no leader, however infallible, can seriously pretend that the unity of Europe can any longer be achieved by force. The danger is that the encouragement of nationalism in the hope of achieving some impossible 'hegemony' may prevent the emergence of a community that can only be based on equality and common consent.

The goal of unity may thus never be achieved and Europe instead of becoming an identifiable object will simply disappear. No *Götterdämmerung* this time (except in the unlikely event of a nuclear war); no heroics; merely a process of adaptation to the ways of one super-power or the other or of both. Indeed the end may be imperceptible. Gradually the high intelligence, the sense of purpose, even the urge of artistic creation will desert these shores. The scientists, the philosophers, the mystics, the engineers, the humanists will find other courts. Greece will be merged in Rome. Life may well be tolerable in our province, But whether it is tolerable or not will not primarily depend on us. On the walls of the Louvre and of Westminster Hall an unseen hand will soon inscribe the words of doom. Authority will be elsewhere. No longer will the quarrelsome nations of Europe have any influence on world events. The very conception of Europe will quickly vanish in the mists of time, along with the great nations that for so long composed it.

If the reader does not mind all this and is only interested in television programmes, pop singers, and the price of whisky, let him proceed no further, If not, let him nevertheless pause for a second and consider the bright future that he plans. For it is by no means certain that a Europe which has been taken over by others will be able to insist on being maintained in the way of life to which she has for so long been accustomed. The province does not control its destiny. The hungry sheep will turn towards those who can feed and support them. In his little backwater, the Englishman might soon get accustomed to his Victory Gin. But it would be sad indeed if it were towards such a future that our young people were marching, as they may be if they see nightmares rather than visions and our old men just dream dreams.

So lest worse befall let us examine together for a moment the European Idea, the glorious conception of the United States of Europe – a new type of unity, an example to the rest of the world, a great hope for peace – and first catch a glimpse of the origin and development of Christendom, or Western Europe or Feranghistan. It is useless to talk about the 'European Idea' or to describe oneself as a 'European' without having at least a notion of its development through the centuries; of what it has meant in the past and therefore of what it may mean in the future. Even those who, like Mr Henry Ford, believe that 'history is bunk' might be inclined to read the few words which follow. If not, they had best begin at Chapter Four, unless indeed 1945 has already been lost in the mists of the past when Chapter Five or even possibly Chapter Six will bring them, so far as possible in a book which must go to press before it appears, into the immediate present.

CHAPTER ONE

*

The Origins of 'Europe'

WHEN the Romans, after their conquest of the Mediterranean basin, began in the second century before Christ, to penetrate beyond the Alps into Gaul, the present France, they found the remains of the loose Gallic community that, a few hundred years previously, had also included Northern Italy, Switzerland, Spain and other parts of the known world, to say nothing of Britain. The Gauls were Celts who had advanced over Western Europe from the East about 1000 BC and who even in the first century BC were being threatened by the German tribes beyond the Rhine, themselves the victims of pressure from other Indo-European tribes advancing from the plains of Central Asia.

The Gauls for the most part lived in substantial clearings in the vast forests which then covered the land. They were a brave, undisciplined, loosely organized, but artistic people who had developed an original civilization, as can be seen from the great monolithic monuments of Carnac in Brittany and Stonehenge in Wiltshire which obviously bore some relation to a worship of the sun. They had a common religion, administered by a special caste, called Druids, embodying, besides human sacrifice, such no doubt satisfying rites as the seasonal communal orgy. This 'old religion' was never entirely stamped out by Christianity and survives today in the shape of many of our popular superstitions, to say nothing of witches' 'covens' and 'black magic' generally. Nevertheless the Gauls did not represent any very stable society as they were highly ungovernable, a characteristic to some extent inherited by the present inhabitants of Gaul.

1

Beyond the Rhine, stretching away towards the Urals over the North European plain, lay the largely impenetrable Hyrcynian wood, at that time inhabited by the much more savage tribes of the Germans and the Saxons – fierce worshippers, in their gloomy wooden temples of Odin and the redoubtable Thor. The climate, nearer to the last Ice Age than we are now, was harsh, the winter long. These barbarians under the pressure of hunger often raided each other. But they also represented a potential threat to the expanding power of Rome.

Caesar in his Gallic War of 57–49 BC (during which he also invaded but did not conquer Celtic Britain) really prevented the German tribes from assuming the mastery of Gaul and thus further threatening the incipient Empire; and when the latter was finally established under Augustus the province as a whole quickly became one of its richest and most settled parts. It was an extraordinary example of a people not only accepting an alien civilization but actually incorporating itself in it. The Gallic notables became Roman citizens. Several later Emperors, including the great Marcus Aurelius, were Gauls. The Gallo-Roman style became a recognizable thing. For three hundred years Gaul, and subsequently Britain too, was a flourishing part of a larger whole. So for that matter was the Rhineland and what is now southern Germany and of course Spain. The law and the language were one. The great network of Imperial communications bound the whole together. The splendid villas and farms, even though run on a form of serfdom, were increasingly productive. The towns were prosperous and civilized. The arts flourished. The forests were slowly cleared. After the attempt to incorporate northern Germany had failed with the defeat of Varus at the battle of the Teutoburger Wald the boundary – the Limes – was set on the Rhine and the Danube. Later, under Trajan, it included Dacia, that is parts of modern Hungary and Rumania. As in the north of Britain the legions established here a row of garrison towns and usually exercised a certain influence beyond it. Within the Limes the Empire held its sway. Geographically, the boundary was remarkably similar to the present Iron Curtain.

2

In the East, Roman domination was also absolute, but here the situation was different. The ancient civilizations of Greece, Egypt and Persia were much older than that of Rome itself. Here Rome was not so much assimilated as imposed. We shall see the effect of this shortly. In the first and second centuries AD, however, the whole Empire was a single organization. As such, it maintained a relationship with the other great civilizations of the time, India (already penetrated by Alexander) and China, though the latter was so distant as to have little effect. Roman galleys touched at Arabian ports and on the coast of Coromandel. They are even thought to have circumnavigated Africa. Only the New World remained totally unknown. Four factors contributed to disrupt this Raj and to bring about the slow decay of the Imperial structure devised by Augustus and carried on by Hadrian, Trajan and the Antonines with its corps of officials, its professional generals, and its system of 'divide and rule'. One was the constant pressure of the barbarians on all the frontiers; the second was the economic weakness resulting from a too highly centralized system; the third was the incompetence of certain Emperors and the manner of their election which came to be based on armed force alone; the fourth was the rise of Christianity which originally weakened the structure and eventually resulted in the division of the Empire.

As a result, in the West the barbarians nearly overturned Rome itself and did incalculable damage in the provinces. Many great cities were destroyed as early as the middle of the third century. The whole system seems to have been saved primarily by the inherent solidity of the institutions coupled with the inability of the barbarians, who were often overawed by the Imperial structure, to form any lasting political entities of their own. But in the West, at any rate, they did finally succeed in abolishing all semblance of Imperial power, which after Diocletian, and in spite of the noble efforts of Julian, steadily declined in importance, Towards the end of the fifth century all was over. Britain and Gaul had been evacuated by the legions. The Goths and the Vandals had twice sacked

3

Rome itself and Italy became an independent kingdom. For a time the invaders respected Roman traditions – some had already been Christianized. In the West the bishops remained in some districts though in Britain they disappeared (as did all Roman influence) for about 150 years after the arrival of the pagan Saxons. The Empire as such only survived in the East, where it lasted for nearly a thousand years, and was for a great deal of the time a really great power. It was Rome, but it was also Greece. Its development does not affect our present story. Only its collapse in 1453 liberated intellectual forces which were partly responsible for what we now call the Renaissance.

Out of the welter of warring tribes that now succeeded to the settled civilization of Rome in the West there gradually emerged, however, a successor to the Imperial power – the Christian Church. The Emperor Constantine had seen the light of Christianity in 312: but he had also placed the centre of the Empire in Byzantium, henceforward Constantinople. 'The new city,' as Fisher says, 'was to be both Christian and Latin. Christian it remained, Latin it soon ceased to be.' In the West, Rome entered into a period of physical if not spiritual decline. Saint Augustine established a Latin orthodoxy bitterly opposed to the Eastern heresy of Arianism which held that the Father was more God-like than the Son: the Bishops of Rome were chiefly responsible for holding up this candle in a world that seemed to be collapsing about their ears. The barbarians chiefly responsible for this collapse in the fifth century were in a general way the Germans, who embraced the Franks, the Vandals, and all the various Goths.

In the early stages of the irruption, which, as we have seen, resulted in separate states being carved out of the Western Roman Empire, the old forms of Imperial administration, the clerks, the writers, even the nobles on their great estates remained. Theodoric the Ostrogoth, the virtual King of Italy, always maintained that he was acting for the Emperor. In Gaul, Aetius mobilized the army that threw back the Huns at the battle of Châlons. But gradually the barbarians formed enduring kingdoms which no longer recognized the Emperor,

4

and the first to do so were the Franks. They were also the first to become Christians, following the example of their king, Clovis, in 496. During this period Britain was, however, over-run by various German tribes who entirely destroyed the Roman civilization of the island and when Saint Augustine arrived in 597 the country was completely pagan and agricultural. Thus the Roman Church was in a way responsible for a second Roman conquest of these islands, and thereafter Britain was again an integral part of European civilization, as it had already been for some four hundred years.

But it was undoubtedly the Franks who provided the nucleus in the West which was eventually to ward off, in the early eighth century, the menace of Islam. Had it not been for Charles Martel's victory over Abdur Rahman in 732 Christianity would probably have disappeared from the whole of Western Europe, as it would have a few years earlier in the East, but for the successful defence of Constantinople by Leo the Isaurian. How was it that this German nucleus was responsible for such a startling victory over the trained and civilized armies of the Muslims which had been driving all before them for the previous century? Because the 'free' Franks, in contrast to the other German tribes, had absorbed the civilization of the Gallo-Romans, and had gradually formed a working alliance with the spiritual descendants in the West of the Roman Empire, in other words the Pope. It was indeed about this time that the thing which came to be known as Christendom or, more properly perhaps as Feranghistan, was born. Charles Martel did indeed refuse the Keys of Saint Peter sent to him by Gregory III, but his successor, Pippin, broke the power of the Lombards in northern Italy and (with the aid of the 'forged decretals' of Constantine) handed over their lands not to the Emperor in Constantinople but to the Bishop of Rome, thus establishing the Papal States, and, basically, the astonishing politico-religious system which was to dominate the rising, the new civilization. For at this time, too, the savage Germans beyond the Rhine had been largely converted to Christianity through the efforts of Frankish and, above all, English monks. King

Pippin was himself anointed by an Englishman – Boniface. England indeed, recovering from her century and a half of paganism, was entering the new community as a founder member. For the definite appearance of a new civilization, however, the West had to wait for the emergence of Pippin's son, the genius who was above all responsible for it – Charlemagne.

This great man who assumed the leadership of the West when he was crowned Emperor by the Pope on Christmas Day AD 800, epitomized the synthesis which was to be at the base of Europe explicitly from then till the Reformation, and implicitly from then till now. By reducing the Germans up to the Elbe and in a general way up to the Vistula and extending his empire south to the Ebro, Charles, in co-operation with the ruler of the Papal States and with a kind of vague suzerainty over a friendly England, created the nucleus of Europe, the Christendom or Feranghistan which, in spite of all subsequent horrors, is still, after close on twelve centuries, an entity, a thing which is identifiable in itself. From Charles' time date the first efforts to establish a reorganized form of learning beginning with a kind of travelling school that went with him even on his campaigns. In these efforts he was assisted by notable English Christians, in particular Alcuin. The contemporary spread of great religious orders like the Benedictines helped also to civilize the barbarous countryside. Also from this time date the legends, like the Song of Roland, which broadened out over the years into a new kind of literature. From his reign, we trace a new form of law, a system for consulting the notables which developed into the Council and eventually into Parliament and finally a new structure of society, known as feudalism, which was the basis of civilized life until the later Middle Ages. In a word there was now engendered, under the stresses of the tribal clashes, a new community. The tradition of the Empire, the zest of the most genial of the barbarians, and the zeal of the Church combined to produce a fusion: Christendom had been born.

The Carolingian Empire was not, it is true, to last long in its new found glory. Not only did it break up physically almost at once, but it was soon subjected to a new wave of barbarian invasion, perhaps the fiercest of all. In the north the Danes appeared on most of the Imperial coasts: in the south the Muslim Saracens. After a wild century and a half the Danes, largely owing to the genius of Alfred, were eventually absorbed in the English society and the Normans, the branch which had established themselves at the mouth of the Seine, quickly adapted themselves to the ways of the weakened Empire and notably to those of the King of the Franks, already known as the King of France, whose very language these Danes had by this time adopted. It was thus in a sense as an agent of the Carolingian conception of Christendom that their leader, William, conquered Britain in 1066 and thereby associated it much more firmly than it had ever been since the Romans with a continental system. If you like, it was in practice a third Roman conquest.

During this time the general idea of Christendom made great progress chiefly owing to the intense activity of the Church and the religious orders and a series of remarkable Popes. The first universities appeared at Bologna, Paris and at Oxford. The first great Romanesque churches and cathedrals went up. The extraordinary First Crusade succeeded in wresting Jerusalem from the Saracens and in turning the Holy Land into a separate Christian state, known to the Franks as 'Outremer'. Fostered by the reforming movement of Cluny a tremendous effort was made to reform the clergy and assert the absolute power of the Vicar of Christ over the merely temporal authority of the Emperor. In the end, in spite of the latter's act of subjection at Canossa, Pope Hildebrand lost his struggle with the temporal power, though a compromise was reached after his death in so far as the investiture of bishops was concerned. But all through this dreadful conflict which lasted for centuries, was never finally settled and ruined the accomplishment of the great conception of Charlemagne, there was a continuing belief (*a*) that there should, in principle, be an authority of some kind in Christendom and (*b*) that that authority must also have a moral or, if you like, a spiritual aspect.

One almost equally unfortunate result of the failure of the

splendid Hohenstauffens from Barbarossa to Frederick II was the consequential failure to establish in the formative period either a German or an Italian nation. Only a loose federation of German and northern Italian feudal principalities and the Papal states emerged – a set-up which more or less lasted till the Franco-Prussian War. At a time indeed when France, England, and later Spain were rapidly emerging as strong monarchies there was no corresponding development in Italy where Frederick II's efforts came to nothing, or north and east of the Alps where a shadowy Emperor was often less important than his nominal vassals. Europe in the thirteenth century was therefore an extraordinary collection of incipient states, bubbling over with new ideas often originating in the newly formed universities, sometimes propagated by the travelling friars, with one religion which, after the extirpation of the Algibenses, was firmly founded on the philosophy of Saint Thomas Aquinas and with above all a sense of unity, even if unity, in diversity, which was chiefly manifested in a common sacred language and in a common acknowledgment, however limited, of a spiritual head.

This system might well have resulted in an even greater sense of European purpose but for two events, the Hundred Years' War between France and England which prevented the formation of some joint dominion in the West, and the Black Death which largely disrupted the developing and changing society. After the middle of the fourteenth century in any case a decline set in. The sense of high purpose which had characterized much of the struggles of the previous century, and which had been expressed in the apocalyptic vision of Dante in his *Divine Comedy* gradually petered out. This decline reached its lowest point when the Papacy, exiled from Rome in 1305, was broken into two, one Pope returning to Rome, the other becoming, at Avignon, almost an agent of the King of France. It was, however, also the beginning of a spiritual rebirth. But while Wycliffe in England and Huss in Bohemia represented genuine reformist tendencies they also challenged the whole conception of the Holy Church Universal. The beginning of the end of the system was at hand. Nationalism received a great impetus with the victories of the French over the English and the inspired leadership of Joan of Arc. New ideas, based on a study of the Greek and Latin classics were also penetrating the West consequent on the fall of Constantinople in 1453. The discovery of the New World enlarged men's horizons. A secular, as opposed to a religious art was spreading from Italy. The fundamental conceptions of Christendom were being challenged from within.

In the ensuing Lutheran Reformation, indeed, the very existence of Christendom was at stake. Luther after publicly associating Papal Rome with Sodom broke with Rome altogether, less perhaps on matters of faith than of authority, and his followers who quickly spread over those parts of Germany which were never part of the Roman Empire set up their own churches, usually dependent on the goodwill of some local ruler. The chief reason for Luther's success in Germany was largely because he had every qualification to be a national hero. 'Not since Barbarossa,' says Fisher, 'had there been a German so typical of his age and race.' Calvin, the Frenchman who settled in Geneva, also quickly obtained an enormous influence in France, no doubt partly for nationalistic reasons. In England there was an even more serious break with the system when Henry VIII failed to obtain a divorce from Katharine of Aragon (the sister of the Emperor) and took the whole kingdom out of communion with Rome. Even so there might conceivably have been some solution based on a reform of the Roman Curia or the development of General Councils had it not been for the decision of one man to reassert the validity both of the Imperial and the Papal idea.

The Emperor Charles V, a Burgundian by descent and a Spaniard by adoption (he was the grandson of Ferdinand and Isabella of Spain), owing to his inheritance, his patience and the circumstances of his age, was the first man for many centuries to attempt to unite Europe by force of arms and to re-establish in some new form the old conception of his predecessor Charlemagne. No one could have been more European, for he talked

9

Spanish to God, French to his friends, Italian to his mistress and German to his horse. Under his dominion were many minor principalities of all racial origins, but his power was chiefly based on the 'new' nation of Spain, then enjoying the boom occasioned by the recent conquest of Mexico and Peru. Attempts to create a united Italian nation at the end of the fifteenth century had crashed with the battle of Fornovo after which Italy was simply a geographical expression and at the mercy of various invaders. Thus with the aid of a reformed Church and a new militant order, the Society of Jesus, the new Emperor really tried to assert the Imperial authority and bring the northern heretics back into the fold, sometimes by diplomacy and sometimes by force. His brother Ferdinand held the Austrian marches and was involved in a desperate struggle with the Turks. It might have been hoped to unite Christendom once again against the infidel.

The attempt failed. The religious Peace of Augsburg of 1555 was a compromise. In the same year, following the example of the Roman Emperor Diocletian, the Emperor abdicated and retired to the monastery of Yuste in the Estremadura. The nation-states of France and England – for such by that time they had become – together with the passionate resistance of the Protestants in the Netherlands, broke the Counter-Reformation. An attempt a few years later to repeat the process by Charles' son Philip II was defeated also, this time by the English in the most celebrated of their victories at sea. The tide had firmly set against all efforts to re-establish any politico-religious unity in Europe, and in fact this ancient conception in its original sense soon went into a long decline. The subsequent furious religious wars in France (which also ended in the compromise of the Edict of Nantes in 1598) did not seriously weaken that country. But the disputed authority in Germany following on the Reformation and the Counter-Reformation had an increasingly frightful effect, and the Thirty Years' War of 1618–48, in which, of course, France and England, and above all Sweden, intervened from time to time to defeat the final efforts of the Europeans in the shape of the House of Hapsburg to exert its

10

authority in Europe as a whole, got completely out of hand, the eventual result being that something like one third of the entire German population perished. Germany (as opposed to Austria) was reduced to such a state that it took her at least two centuries to recover. Cardinal Richelieu had lengthened the war considerably by his astute diplomacy and after the Peace of Westphalia, which ended the struggle, there was no doubt which was the strongest and indeed, at that time, much the largest country in Europe: it was France. The attempts of France to exercise a hegemony and the reactions to these attempts were the chief motive force in European diplomacy during the next 175 years.

From this point onwards the European Idea as such lost much of its old appeal and may be said to have gone underground. The Peace of Westphalia had after all given the final sanction to the new nation-state, the body owing allegiance to no one, which, in the shape of England at any rate, had really appeared with the Reformation. The potential European anarchy to which this phenomenon obviously gave rise was tempered to some extent by the increasingly civilized behaviour of the governing classes, by the so-called 'Republic of Letters' and by the acceptance of a rudimentary system of international law. But it was anarchy all the same. No principle, religious or other, lay at the back of the interminable eighteenth-century wars. It was simply a case of every nation for itself and the devil take the hindmost. Had the Turk still been a menace either one great European power or the other would still have not scrupled to make an alliance with him. Mercifully no outside power, save Russia, was in a position to interfere in European affairs: and Russia was only just beginning under Peter the Great and Catherine to acquire the necessary skills without which she could scarcely be a menace to anybody. So the struggle had no catastrophic consequences.

Its chief feature was the highly successful rôle of the first nation-state, Britain, small in numbers but well placed geographically in playing off one side against the other and thus never allowing a hegemony on the mainland to be achieved.

From the Reformation onwards Britain had gradually established that 'special and separate' position as regards the mainland which she successfully maintained right down till 1961. Marlborough's wars were the first example of the triumph of this policy. The great Roi Soleil had been successfully 'contained', and the Peace of Utrecht in 1715 marked the beginning of the world rôle of these islands. Under cover of this insurance Britain had indeed entered the race for expansion overseas which had been begun by Spain after the discovery of the new world. In the sixteenth century English explorers and pirates disputed the monopoly of Spain; in the seventeenth English Puritans established several colonies in North America; in the eighteenth the East India Company was formed. In America and India Britain came into natural conflict with France. Largely because of the latter's preoccupations with European hegemony, she won. By 1763 the French had lost Canada and were largely out of India. They had their revenge a few years later when the English North American colonies rebelled and, to a great extent owing to French help, asserted their independence. But the great French chance to assert her dominion over Europe and at the same time to prevent England from playing her game any longer came with the Napoleonic Wars.

The French Revolution, child of French and British philosophers, was in a sense an effort to get away from the anarchy of nation-states. Nor in spite of the early chauvinism was it devoid of European content, though its leaders had of course nothing in common with the medieval system of Emperor and Pope. There was indeed a genuine belief that the new political principle, invented in France, should and would be adopted by other European states; though of course they were also thought of as being of universal validity. And when under the leadership of the great Corsican, French soldiers stormed into Italy, Germany and Spain they still believed that they were 'liberating' the local populations who would all soon join some enormous European Federation of which Paris would naturally be the capital. When he had himself crowned Emperor by the Pope in 1804, Napoleon himself was, however, going back to a less revolutionary and much more traditional solution. Consciously repeating the gesture of Charlemagne he demonstrated the continuous strength of the basic European Idea, even though all history had shown so far that force alone could not successfully put it into practice.

Once again Britain foiled this plan. On sea and on land this relatively small island produced an enormous effort of its own and in addition supplied to a large extent the sovereigns – the *'cavalerie de Saint Georges'* – that kept the anti-French coalition going. Once again, too, she saw the final success of her instinctive fight. The man who might very well have established an enduring European empire ended up in Saint Helena where he is supposed to have observed, quite shrewdly, that a hundred years after his death Europe would be either Americanized or Cossack. But in the meantime it was evident that the nineteenth was to be Britain's century. Secure across the Channel, she could concentrate on her vast overseas expansion. First exponent of the industrial, as opposed to the political revolution she would pursue a completely nationalistic policy and, as Canning said, if necessary 'call in the New World to redress the balance of the old.' Never was there less talk in political circles of European unity. Certainly in Britain there were few who even thought of such an old-fashioned idea. And yet the idea persisted, intellectually at any rate as we shall shortly see in Chapter Three.

Politically, one of its manifestations had been the so-called Holy Alliance, the system devised by the Tsar Alexander to combat revolutionary force by inducing Christian rulers to combine to preserve the *status quo*. Although it was conceived by a non-European and was to some extent justifiably denounced as a 'sublime combination of mysticism and nonsense' it did represent an effort to temper the excesses of the nation-state and establish a kind of European authority. Britain did not join, but Castlereagh associated his country with a parallel Great Power Diet of Britain, Russia, Austria and Prussia designed to resist Bonapartist tendencies in the ex-enemy, France. Even this system, however, soon collapsed under the

13

pressure of the new nationalist movements all over Europe, and though there was later a vague notion of some 'Concert of Europe' it was not a tangible expression of any real European Idea. Nationalism therefore had free rein. It produced a general revolution in 1848 which might conceivably have resulted in a democratic or indeed socialistic Europe but which was suppressed by the existing states. Out of it came the Second Empire in France and the Second German Reich. France had, however, shot her bolt and it was in Bismarck's achievement that lay the germ of the last attempt to apply force to the unification of the Continent.

This was not at first apparent. After the Franco-German War of 1870 and the Congress of Berlin of 1878 most people thought that Europe had reached a period of stability. It was certainly becoming increasingly prosperous. There was reason to believe that the astonishing economic progress and the great network of railways would, in accordance with the principles of Cobden, gradually bind the nation-states together so that some kind of political union would in the course of time emerge. Moreover, the amazing expansion of Europe was well under way. The techniques devised by Western man seemed miraculous to the primitive and astonishingly desirable even to the ancient nations of the world. In India the British took over from another foreign Raj and ruled the sub-continent for nearly as long. Africa was partitioned; the Middle East entirely dominated; China came under Western influence, as did most of South-East Asia. Of the ancient nations only Japan, Siam and (for a long time) Abyssinia avoided what was virtually colonial status. There seemed every reason to suppose that Europe would gain enormously by co-operating. It was not to be. The European nation-states advanced steadily towards their doom.

The so-called First World War can now be seen for what it was, namely, the start of the Third European Civil War (1914–45), the first being the Thirty Years' War and the second the French Revolutionary and Napoleonic Period. All these wars were concerned with the basic question, how was Europe to be run? Should there be some central authority, and, if so, what?

All three had started on the basic assumption that this authority, to all intents and purposes, could only be one of the new nation-states, the invention and the bane of Christendom. In a sense the 1914 disaster was evitable. It may even be said to have been a terrible mistake. But the underlying causes were such that it was probably in the long run inevitable, For nearly twenty years the Second German Reich (the first being, of course, the 'Holy Roman Empire of the German Nation') had been challenging, implicitly, and later explicitly, the thalassocracy of Britain. The two Central Powers were really a coalition which wanted, instinctively, to achieve a mastery of Europe first by pushing back the Russians (regarded as an alien menace) and then by forcing Britain to abandon her century-long policy of divide and rule. Britain, as usual, was found on the side of the weaker combination. An appalling struggle followed. After each side had lost many millions, American intervention was necessary to tip the scale in favour of the Allies. But the Treaty of Versailles did not produce a settlement in the sense of solving the vital question of where in Europe authority should lie. Indeed it produced a new crop of small independent nation-states dependent for their salvation on one of the larger powers or the other. Nor had Germany been eliminated as a potential force. The Second Reich was no more but the German Republic remained to a large extent the mistress of its destinies. Russia had disappeared from the European scene. Finally the American troops went back to America and the United States, perhaps regretting its first step outside, retired into its own powerful province. In spite of the proclaimed total victory of the Allies the 1914–18 struggle really ended in a draw.

Since the vital political problem had obviously not been solved, it was clear that there would, at some time, be another attempt to solve it. The great depression, by creating large-scale unemployment in Germany and Britain precipitated the issue. A wave of collective hysteria in Germany produced a man whose ability was only equalled by his malice. The Civil War was resumed, this time by Hitler's simple will to power. It was the old effort to unite Europe by force of arms, and it very nearly succeeded. But when the even more frightful struggle was over it was seen that a prostrate and devastated Christendom had been divided between two outside powers, one nearly and the other distantly related. Did this prove that the millenary idea was futile, if not actually pernicious? Was Europe really dead?

If there is any conclusion to be drawn from a hasty backward glance it is this. The European Idea, historically speaking, has never been fully applied. Since the third century, when it was simply a part of the Roman Empire, and for a brief moment under Charlemagne, Europe has never physically been one. Nevertheless the urge to unite it, though it may vary in intensity, has never disappeared, and appears to give rise from time to time to struggles which are invariably self-destructive. Are we to conclude that the Europeans, like the Ancient Greeks will never accept a hegemony but will ultimately submit themselves to a 'Federator'? They have indeed reached the point where, unless they can peacefully combine, they may be obliged to do so. The present chance of unity may well be the last. Two potential Federators are now politically present in the middle of our small sub-continent. So let us here examine Europe's relationship with the one super-power and the other.

CHAPTER TWO

*

The Daughter and the Cousin

WE have seen how America emerged from her secular isolation in 1917 and how in 1945 she prevented her parent from dying of the near mortal sickness which had caused the third 'Thirty Years' War'. Why did she feel impelled to do so? Whence came the almost instinctive urge to support one side in this civil war against the other and thus to settle it? To answer these questions we must trace briefly the history of her own development.

The European, chiefly English, colonies in North America date from the early seventeenth century. The French established themselves in Quebec and beyond about the same time. For over a century each of these colonies depended entirely on its own metropolis. (New York was taken over by the English from the Dutch in 1664.) A great deal of the time of the colonists was taken up with Indian Wars and the clearing of the forests. The eighteenth-century struggles between Britain and France spread to the New World. As we have already seen the British finally won and imposed their dominion over Canada in 1763. But the French had a partial revenge when, with their important assistance, the English colonies rebelled and declared their independence in 1776. Thenceforward a new power was in existence, while in the north Canada developed more slowly as part of a larger whole. This, however, did not mean that America became less provincial. On the contrary, independence for many years encouraged provincialism; and from Washington onwards the American Presidents and Congresses were largely occupied with asserting, behind the shield of the

Royal Navy, their separate innocence, avoiding 'entangling alliances' and generally denouncing the sins and follies of an all-powerful Europe, more particularly, in the nineteenth century, an all-powerful Britain.

However, the physical development of the new continent proceeded apace. The receding frontiers became an obsession and the 'frontier' mentality came to dominate even the more settled parts of the United States. Soon the Alleghenies were crossed in numbers and the Great Plains were developed. In 1803 Louisiana was acquired from the French. In 1804 the Rockies were reached. In the 1840s the West Coast began to be organized. In 1842 came the final boundary demarcation with Canada. Texas joined the Union in 1845. In 1869 the railway stretched across the continent. The geographical limits had been reached. The shy and gangling potential giant stood revealed.

But this tremendous effort demanded more and more men, far more than the Americans could themselves provide. In the late eighteenth and early nineteenth centuries immigrants first arrived from Ulster and the Highlands of Scotland, largely ruined after the English wars. But the first great influx came from Ireland in the 'hungry forties', and particularly after the potato famine in 1848. It is thought that about one and a half million Irish arrived about this time, many in terrible conditions of distress. Soon the Germans, some fleeing dictatorship at home, began crossing the Atlantic as did many Scandinavians. Then there was the great wave from Italy and to some extent from Iberia as well; later from Poland and from Western Russia, mostly Jews. Every year the immigrant ships of the Cunard and other lines set out from Liverpool, Bremen and Naples packed with immigrants – 'the wretched refuse' as the Statue of Liberty proudly announces 'of our teeming shore'. Only the outbreak of the First World War put a temporary end to the traffic, and in 1922 the quota was introduced and the great *Völkerwänderung* came to an end. The population of the United States had risen from four million in 1790, seventeen million in 1840, to 110 million in 1922. The Americans had absorbed all they could profitably absorb. The continent was full.

Full of what? Of people of predominantly Western European stock. People who, however much they might have fought each other in the past, nevertheless shared certain ancient memories and ideals. People who for the most part possessed the same restless energy; the same tradition of applied science and mechanical ability; the same practical outlook on the world; the same desire for freedom. They could be – many of them were – divided by old loyalties and feuds. (That between the Irish and the English survives to this day.) But they could also combine and intermarry and learn English easily for the simple reason that they nearly all had, in the last resort, and in their unconscious selves, the same cultural background. Beethoven, Copernicus, Newton, Harvey, Laplace, Curie, Marconi, Einstein spoke an international language. They were the result of an extraordinary cross-fertilization. The same seminal ideas often appeared in many parts of the area at the same time. The American was thus increasingly an amalgam. The 'melting pot' had worked. The Daughter had finally grown up. What kind of relationship would she now entertain with the parent culture?

All family relationships are difficult. The parent is seldom conscious of the entirely separate personality of the child. When America emerged from provincial status she came of age. A separate personality was formed. For a long time it was still dominated by the formidable parent, but the First World War hastened the inevitable process of liberation, and when the Second World War arrived the shoe was rather on the other foot. Nevertheless Americans are still conscious of their origins, both geographical and cultural. They continue to come in numbers to seek out their relations and their old families and homes. They feel, many of them, that they are still part of Western Europe and it was perhaps the suspicion that if Christendom were physically united under an authoritarian German, and more especially under Nazi domination, they might be excluded or at least have a less close relationship with the parent that resulted in their intervention in two world wars. This instinct is justified; for as we have seen they *are*, in a way, what Western Europeans would be if they ever were united.

Will they one day no longer feel this urge? Will they not come to Europe more than Europeans will come to America? Perhaps though this is not certain. Americans are now a nation at least as distinct from Europe as one European nation is from another. Some would say that they are more distinct. Is it possible that they will lose all real sense of identity? Might they even one day repudiate the Mother? Could they contemplate being equally close to, say, India or Japan?

This seems very doubtful. In the first place there is something special in the very soil and climate of Western Europe so far as its own civilization is concerned. It is by no means certain that the basic values of this civilization can flourish in an alien atmosphere. Certainly it does not look as if they would be adopted by the older civilizations of the world. There the products of these values are adopted, from boiler suits to the atom bomb, but not the values themselves. The idea that the individual can and should have rights that are inherent in himself and the means of asserting them is not understood or accepted, hardly even in India which has been exposed to Western influence for two centuries or more. Even the material manifestation of Western civilization, namely, industrialization, is not normally indigenous elsewhere. The thoughts, the inventions, what the Germans call the *Fingerspitzgefühl*, usually have to be imported if efficiency is to be maintained. Even America herself is not exempt from this apparent tendency. It is probably true that the bulk of the West's inventive capacity is still in the Old World and that the chief strength of the New lies in the large-scale development of such ideas and inventions. This may not always be so, but since the civilization of America – and indeed of Australia – is one which was taken up and translated to what was in effect virgin territory, it is very different from the position in such very ancient lands as China where the adoption of many Western standards is in some ways an excuse for the revival of national values.

America, then, is a part of the West which, except as the result of some catastrophe, can hardly be separated from it. As she progresses towards maturity she becomes less resentful of certain attitudes of the parent and indeed has probably now reached the point where she no longer cares very much. But she cannot ignore the parent. In 1945–8 she realized she could not allow the Mother to collapse. In 1965 it is rather a question whether she would prefer Western Europe to come to live in America's attic or to set up permanently on her own. Even if the parent takes this last course there is no reason why relations should be bad. Indeed they are likely to improve. The 'special relationship' will endure whatever happens. Towards the Third World the Feranghis on both sides of the Ocean can hardly help presenting a rather similar face. Western techniques may be, indeed are being, employed effectively in many other countries; but the pragmatical approach, the application of reason to modern sociological problems, the constant desire to innovate, are things which are likely to persist in the whole 'Atlantic' world.

The relationship of Western Europe with Russia is very different but there are points of resemblance too. In the first place the Russians have white skins and are ultimately of the same racial origin as the Franks. Their language is Indo-European: they react in general to the same stimuli; they take more easily than most to the processes of industrialization. Moreover, for the last three or four hundred years they have been in close contact with Europe. Ever since the reforms of Peter the Great their upper classes and (in the nineteenth century) their intelligentsia were profoundly affected by Western philosophy, manners and literature. It may further be said with truth that in the nineteenth century Russian music and literature were actually a part of Western civilization. Some masterpieces are indeed kindred works to those of the great Western European artists in a sense that those of Chinese, Persian or Indian authors definitely are not. Nor can the greatest Russian authors be properly described as in any way provincial. On the contrary, their works were authoritative products of a civilization which shares many essential characteristics with that of Western Europe. Indeed between the Napoleonic Wars and the Revolution in 1917 Russian literature and music was not derivative, as was, for the most part, that of America during this period. There was then an intellectual ferment in Russia which was not paralleled on the other side of the Atlantic where all efforts were chiefly concentrated in the physical formation of the new continental state.

But if until the 1917 Revolution the two civilizations of the West and the East had much in common there was still a great deal that separated them. Ever since the final split of 1054 the two Churches of Rome and Byzantium had been entirely separate. While Christendom was being formed the Slavs were pagan. Christianity came from the West to the Poles and Czechs, Hungarians and Slovenes in the ninth and tenth centuries. Russia was, however, only Christianized in 988, and when the missions arrived they came to Kiev from Constantinople. After the fall of the city in 1453 the Patriarch of Moscow was one of the heads of the Eastern Church, but the Tsar became in his own estimation the incarnation of the Roman Empire in its Eastern form which had lasted for a thousand years. 'Holy Russia' dates from then. A separate civilization was about to emerge.

Suspicion and indeed fear of the West were endemic in this civilization. For centuries the Lithuanian and then the Polish Catholic kings had dominated, with varying fortune, the lands between the Vistula and the Don. Russia which had freed herself from the rule of the Tartars and the 'Golden Horde' was formed largely by resistance to this challenge. After the Poles, the Swedes attempted to conquer these lands. Finally the Russian power emerged and after Peter the Great entered in the eighteenth century into direct relations with the major powers of Christendom. But this relationship was always different in kind from the relationship between the Western powers themselves. Russia, they used to say in the eighteenth-century Chancelleries, was always too late, and when she did come she was too strong. Glorious buildings were put up by the Italian architect, Rastrelli, and others in St Petersburg and Moscow itself, but few of the ideas of the French Encyclopaedists and none of those of the French Revolution penetrated far into Musscovy. Suspicion of the West was ineradicable. In spite of the freeing of the serfs, the experiment with a Duma after 1858 and the beginning of industrialization after about 1863, Russia remained an auto- cracy until the Revolution; and though she then (after a period of anarchy) went ahead with the industrial process – perhaps more slowly than if there had been no Revolution at all – she was, under Lenin and more especially Stalin, essentially an autocracy still. Djugashvili, the Georgian and the 'spoilt priest', was very conscious of his Imperial descendancy.

For a long time too even after she had dealt with the Poles and the Swedes Russia feared the West. The Napoleonic in- vasion had been an invasion by Europe itself. In the Grande Armée most continental European countries were represented. Moscow, the holy city, was burnt. The Russian people in- stinctively believed that the West was hostile to the Motherland, to the 'Rodina': for their part the West were conscious of the formation of a potential colossus which might one day be a menace. The Russians bivouacked in the Champs Elysées in 1814 were regarded as a warning, and though throughout the nineteenth century it was rather Russia's weaknesses which were exposed than her power, the huge armies of the Tsar were always present in the minds of Europe's statesmen.

In 1917 the Germans were in command of much of Russia. Had they won the war they would undoubtedly have colonized the Ukraine. During the chaos that followed the collapse both of Germany and of Russia, the Allies tried to intervene on the side of the Counter Revolution, and were repulsed, not so much by the Revolution itself as by patriotic and anti-foreign feeling. The Soviet Union was thereafter for many years in total isola- tion and tried (successfully) to industrialize itself without foreign aid. The Russian people believed that if they were success- ful in this the West would attack them. How right they were was shown in 1941. Again most of the nations of Europe were represented in Hitler's army, Italy and Spain quite substan- tially. This time the balance was turned by American and British support, but not before Russia, partly through her own fault, had lost seventeen million men and had in any case seen her citizens subjected, in the name of the German people to barbarities which almost defeat the human imagination.

The relationship of Russia to the West, must therefore, in the nature of things, be ambivalent. She is obviously more suspicious of Europe than is America for whom she entertains a kind of hate-love. For she fears, no doubt wrongly but quite understandably, that, even without American active support, Europe might one day, under German leadership, resume her secular eastern movement. Prevention of German unity for as long as possible will therefore almost certainly continue to be a main feature of Russian policy. If she can combine this with successful efforts to undermine the unity of Western Europe that will be even better. By such means she will always hope to divide the Mother and the Daughter. Whether she will ever be able to get Mother, whatever her follies, to come and join her in another family is, however, open to the gravest doubt. Whatever we may do or say, the Russians are more 'foreign' than the Americans. It is not only just the language. It has little to do with the fact that since 1917 they have adopted as their political philosophy a Western heresy which now shows distinct signs of inadequacy both on the moral and on the material fronts. It is rather the whole Russian attitude to life.

Thus it is probable that any effort to solve the Russian problem by direct means, whether it were by the Germans seeking to employ the American power by one means or another to eject the Soviet Union from the eastern part of Europe or (conceivably) by the French to use the Russian power to persuade the Americans to evacuate Germany, if they were ever seriously pursued, would both miscarry. Indeed either would be disastrous. For the first would awaken the profoundest ancestral fears of the Russian people and perhaps even provoke a kind of hysteria which might have catastrophic consequences: while the second would run the gravest risk of ultimately subjecting the Mother to the domination of the Cousin.

We can thus legitimately conclude that the future of Europe depends first of all on the establishment of the right relationship between Western Europe and America, and then of an understanding between the two super-powers of our modern world which would enable German reunification to take place, at long last, in 'peace and freedom'. How can we best prepare for such a happy event, which is certainly not for today and maybe not for many years? Only by making progress with the idea of a real European unification. It is possible to imagine, for instance, that under outside pressure perhaps, including the rise of China, some understanding will be reached which will not involve the reconstitution of a centralized German state of eighty million people (*ein Reich, ein Volk, ein Führer*) but rather an association of the various German-speaking peoples within the framework of a greater whole. Some day, no doubt, the American Army will go home to America and the Russian Army to Russia. But only when it is evident that no danger will arise thereby to either super-state. Before all this is even conceivable Europe must begin to express an individuality – an autonomy, if you will – of its own and thus at least provide a framework within which the Germans may one day be reunified, and this can only begin to happen if the basic problem is solved of Britain's relationship with the incipient union across the Channel. Only too when this comes about in agreement with the powerful Daughter, that is to say after building up the institutions which will join the two halves of what, as we have seen, is after all a common civilization.

There is no need why the Cousin should fear such a development. There is no need why she should believe that her own separate identity or individuality should thereby be endangered. Europe, if it is ever formed, will not be an empire in the old fashioned sense – the sense of nationality is far too persistent among the ancient states which will compose it. If it is formed it is more likely to be a new form of association altogether, open, as always with Western man, to the so-called 'wind of change'. There should be no internal forces making for expansion. There is no reason why it should not have the friendliest relations with the Great Power to the East. Only if it remains a collection of quite independent small and medium powers is it likely to be a focus of dissension or a cold war battle-front. Besides, it is not only a question of 'Western' ideas penetrating and perhaps convulsing the Soviet Union. There are certain Russian ideas, resulting from the long and separate existence of Russia and its roots in Byzance, which might also profitably be adopted by the West. It has been said, and rightly, that whereas the Russian people have little liberty or indeed equality, they do have fraternity, which, as a political virtue, is not altogether a dominant consideration with the Franks.

So let us when we consider the greatest problem of our day, namely, the stark 'confrontation' between Russia and America, in other words, the division of Christendom imposed by the nuclear 'balance of terror', always grasp the fact that only the emergence of a peaceful Europe in close association with the New World but also holding out her hand to Russia, can end the cold war and prepare for the day when some kind of disarmament will be possible. As between the Daughter and the Cousin the Mother has a real rôle to play, provided that she can overcome her inherent suicidal tendencies. Many remedies have been put forward over the years for curing this tendency and they will be examined in the following chapter.

CHAPTER THREE

*

Efforts to Cure Europe's Suicidal Tendencies by the Use of Reason

EVER since about the year 1300, that is to say from the point in time in the later Middle Ages when the Carolingian conception began to falter and the nation-state was about to be born (a tendency lamented by Dante), plans appear designed to check the self-destructive instincts of the Feranghis and to induce them to unite for the good of all. The first, on record, suitably enough, was that of Pierre Dubois, a French lawyer who observed that peace could only be preserved if there were institutions to preserve it and that such institutions must be firmly based on the principle of arbitration. The various monarchs should come together and reach some kind of agreement to this end. The King of France should take the lead. But the supreme arbiter might well be the Pope. Nobody seems to have paid any serious attention to these proposals and the next plan, so far as we know, was put forward in 1464 by a certain Marigny, a French refugee at the Court of King Podriebad of Bohemia, an able elected monarch who wanted to become Emperor and who, as a Hussite, was not in favour of the Pope. Podriebad's eventual plan was for an alliance of states which would all combine against what we would now call the aggressor, or against any one of these members who refused arbitration, which would be obligatory on membership of the group. A few states agreed but the scheme came to nothing owing to the opposition of the French.

By the end of the fifteenth century national frontiers were

27

becoming more fixed. The Renaissance and the Reformation both led to greater independence from Rome and signs of the beginning of nationalism and colonialism were soon to appear. Equally it was at this time that the policy of the 'balance of power' in Europe made its first appearance. Nevertheless, alongside the empirical diplomacy of kings (pursued by a mixture of wars, alliances and marriages), lawyers and thinkers still dreamt of uniting the Continent. Thus for example, the Spanish Jesuit, Suarez, published in 1612 his *Tractatus de legibus et Deo legislatore*, in which he says that 'although every state – republic or monarchy – is in itself a perfect community composed of its own members, it is no less true that each state considered in its relationship with the human race is part in some way of a universal community. It is indispensable that they have a law to direct them and put them in their place in this sort of community or society.' The great Dutch lawyer Grotius, in his *De Jure belli et pacis* (1625), speaks of the need to 'establish between the Christian powers a sort of body, with its assemblies, where the litigations would be judged by those amongst them not involved, so as to find a means of forcing the parties to reconcile themselves in reasonable conditions.' In 1623 Emeric Crucé, priest and teacher, published in Paris *Le Nouveau Cyné, ou Discour des Occasions et Moyens d'établir une Paix Générale et la Liberté du commerce par tout le monde*. Crucé is the first to emphasize the importance of trade between nations, and also the first to include non-Christian states in his plan. He proposed a permanent assembly in Venice of the ambassadors of all the kings.

The influence of all of these ideas was negligible. The best known plan and the first to emanate from statesmen rather than thinkers was the 'Grand Design' of Henry IV of France and his Minister, Maximilian de Bethune, Duke of Sully (1559–1641). Details of the Grand Design are given in Sully's *Œconomies royales*, where it is attributed to King Henry. In fact it seems likely that Henry's own plan was limited to a Protestant alliance to contain Spain and Austria, in connection with which Sully was at one time sent to London to negotiate with Elizabeth I.

But the earlier versions of the *Œconomies royales* make no mention of the Grand Design, and since it is unlikely that Sully would have omitted to mention such an important project if it was genuinely his master's idea, it is more probable that the plan is his own inserted later when he rewrote his memoirs in retirement.

Sully's plan for a *République très chrétienne* was revolutionary. The first and essential prerequisite was a united Germany. Europe would then be divided into fifteen supposedly equal states: the Holy See, Germany, France, Spain, England, Hungary, Bohemia, Poland, Denmark, Sweden, Lombardy, Venice, the Italian Republic (to include all the Italian states except the Holy See, Lombardy and Venice), the Belgian Republic (Belgium and the Netherlands) and the Helvetic Republic (which would include also Franche-Comté, Alsace and the Tyrol). A single religion was desirable, and no more than three religions (Catholic, Calvinist, Lutheran) permissible. The Turks would be permitted to join if converted to Christianity. The *République très chrétienne* was to be headed by a *Conseil très chrétien* composed of forty members appointed for a term of three years: four from each of the larger countries and two from each of the smaller ones. The Council would sit each year in a different city (Sully lists them) and would have full powers to arbitrate in disputes between the members. There would in addition be six provincial councils which would hear cases in the first instance. The *Conseil très chrétien* would be supported by a European Army of one hundred thousand infantrymen, twenty-five thousand cavalry and one hundred and twenty cannon. The provision of soldiers and support costs would be shared among the nations. It was a strange mixture of realism and fantasy. In particular Sully's belief that Europe could be divided up more or less artificially was naïve, and his assertion that the fifteen states would be of equal strength quite unrealistic.

The first Englishman to play with the idea of a United Europe was William Penn the founder of Pennsylvania. In 1693, already in America, Penn published his *Essay on the Present and Future Peace of Europe by the Establishment of a European Diet,*

Parliament and State. His plan was closer to that of Crucé than to Sully's since it postulated no new order in Europe. But it contained one important and significant new element: the Assembly of the United Europe would take its decisions by a three-fourths majority under a voting system weighted according to the demographic and economic importance of the various countries. Thus Germany would have twelve votes, France, Spain, Russia and Turkey ten each, Italy eight, England six, and so on – a total of ninety votes in all. Debates would take place in Latin and French, and decisions would be enforced by a European Army paid for by the country doing wrong. But Penn's whole plan, like that of his predecessors, depended completely on the voluntary agreement of the monarchs concerned, and this despite the fact that he had undoubtedly read Locke's *Essay on Government* (1690) which first put forward the thesis that political and social progress must depend rather upon the will of the people.

The eighteenth century was the Age of Reason, and one might therefore have expected it to produce all kinds of 'European' schemes. The writers and thinkers of the eighteenth century were, it is true, very international in outlook, but paradoxically the ease with which literature and thought crossed national frontiers at that time meant that they saw little purpose in physically uniting Christendom. The attitude of Montesquieu is probably fairly typical. A much travelled man, he accepted completely that 'all the states depend one upon the other. France has need of the wealth of Poland and Muscovy just as Guyenne has need of Brittany and Anjou. Europe is a state composed of several provinces.' He therefore saw no need to build special machinery to prove this fact.

Leibnitz, writing at the very beginning of the century certainly advocated European unity, but in a form of the return to the Holy Roman Empire, where Europe, united under Pope and Emperor, would use its combined forces to bring Christianity to the rest of the world. During almost the whole of the century the only place where one finds the European Idea taken up in a more sophisticated form is in the writing of the Abbé de Saint-

Pierre (1658–1743). He had met Leibnitz when the latter was in Paris, and they subsequently corresponded for some time, but their ideas of Europe differed greatly. The Abbé had been present at the signing of the Treaty of Utrecht which ended the War of the Spanish Succession in 1713, and he chose this moment to publish his *Projet pour Rendre la Paix Perpetuelle en Europe*. It seems to have been little read, until in 1720 Saint-Pierre published a shortened version. His plan consisted of five points: (1) a perpetual alliance between sovereigns, (2) the submission of the sovereigns to the decisions of a European Senate, (3) joint financing of the alliance, (4) collective action against those who fail to follow the rules of the alliance and who would be made to pay the costs of the resulting wars, and (5) the amendment of the five points and changes of frontier to be possible only on unanimous agreement. The European Senate, sitting at either Strasbourg or Dijon, would have both legislative and judicial powers, and would consist of forty members. All states with populations exceeding 1,200,000 would have equal voting rights, and smaller states would have to join together so as to reach this total. Voting would be by a simple majority, but decisions would have to be ratified after six months by a two-thirds majority. Each state would be limited to an army of six thousand men in time of peace, and in wartime a European Army of five hundred thousand would be raised, and commanded by a single general, who could not be a member of any ruling house.

The Abbé de Saint-Pierre's proposals were a real step forward since for the first time they made it clear that the prerequisite of collective security is the acceptance of the rule of law. Yet the scheme was still totally dependent on the agreement of sovereign nations. For this it was strongly criticized by, amongst others, Jean-Jacques Rousseau who published in 1756 a summary of the Abbé's *Projet de paix perpetuelle*. He thought the plan had great merit but could only be workable if based upon the agreement of peoples instead of sovereigns, who were by their very nature greedy of power, imperialistic in their relations with other states and despotic in the conduct of domestic affairs. Thus revolution in the internal structure of the states had to come about first, and even Rousseau is strangely reluctant to say that the risks involved would be justified.

The first person indeed to appeal directly to the people and not to sovereigns was the great Jeremy Bentham. One chapter of his *Principles of International Law* (written in 1798 but not published until 1839) is devoted to a 'Plan for Universal and Perpetual Peace.' Bentham took his argument one step beyond Rousseau, and maintained that European unity was positively in the interest of the people. He advocated the reduction of armaments, the establishment of an international assembly and tribunal (Bentham invented the word 'international'), free trade, the liberty of the press, and the abandonment of all colonies since they were financial liabilities, prevented free trade by the preferential systems they involved and were inevitable bones of contention between the European states. The appeal was evidently to interest as well as to reason, but the plan was unrealistic in its belief that moral sanctions would in the main be sufficient to enforce the laws of the new Europe.

Bentham was writing shortly after the French Revolution. It is hardly surprising that he lays such stress on the rôle of the people rather than of kings. Indeed the 'European' thinkers of the time felt that the French Revolution, by replacing the sovereign by popular control, must inevitably bring European unity a step nearer. Nothing was farther from the truth. True the Convention by a decree of 11 November 1792, promised 'help and fraternity to all peoples who wish to recover their liberty', but its ambitions to begin with were more nationalistic than European. Napoleon, however, had very definite European ambitions. Writing to Cardinal Fesch in 1806 he observed: 'I have not succeeded to the throne of Louis XIV, but to that of Charlemagne.' And though his chosen method of uniting Europe was the primitive one of force, he nevertheless derived his sovereignty from the people and not from divine right, and carried with him throughout Europe the general ideas of the rights of man. In his exile in St Helena, writing his *Memorial*, he said: 'I cannot think that after my fall and the disappearance of my system, there will be in Europe any other basis for

32

equilibrium than the agglomeration or confederation of great peoples.' Elsewhere he recommended to his successor to reunite Europe in indissoluble federal bonds. And indeed the fall of Napoleon did mean a decline in the conception of human rights, and the reversion to the nation-state and (except in England) to absolute hereditary monarchy.

We must now take some account of the ideas of the great German philosopher, Emmanuel Kant. Kant had undoubtedly read Saint-Pierre and like him insists above all on the rule of law. But he also insists that laws must be based on the people and not imposed upon them from above or without. In his *Philosophical Project for Perpetual Peace* (1795) – and indeed in all his works – he insists on the supremacy of man-made laws over the laws of nature in relations between states as well as between individuals:

'In the eyes of reason there is no other means whereby states, considered in their reciprocal relationships, can abandon the state of war, in which they are restrained by no law, than to renounce, as to individuals, the anarchic liberty of the savage – the state of nature – in order to submit to the constraint of public laws and thus form a State of nations which will ever grow and eventually embrace all the peoples of the earth.'

Kant inevitably rejects the right of kings to govern their people arbitrarily and equally rejects any idea of a universal monarchy. Law must be based upon a 'federation of free states'. But he accepts that for all practical purposes this is impossible and suggests as a first step a simple confederation between sovereign nations each of which may withdraw at any time. No indication is given of what the second and subsequent steps might be.

A little later the Comte de Saint-Simon devoted much of his great energy to attempts to 'reorganize European society'. In 1814 he published *De la Réorganisation de la Société Européenne, ou de la Nécéssité et des Moyens de rassembler les Peuples de l'Europe en un Seul Corps Politique, en conservant à chacun son*

Indépendence Nationale. He criticizes his predecessors for their acceptance of the absolutism which dominated all Europe until the English and then the French Revolutions, and insists that any union must be founded upon parliamentary control. Thus the first step and the cornerstone of the new Europe would be the union of England and France. Coming from one so interested in technical detail his proposals are strangely vague. The new union would have a hereditary king at its head, whose powers would be strictly limited. There would be a *grand parlement européen* having two houses, one nominated by the kings and the other and more important one elected by all citizens able to read and write and having certain property qualifications. Each million citizens would elect one merchant, one scientist, one lawyer and one administrator, all for a ten-year term. Initially on account of its greater experience of these matters, England would have two-thirds of the seats. No mention is made at all of the rôle of the Parliament in external affairs, but it would be empowered to undertake public works in the general interest and would control education throughout the union. This would seem to suggest an almost unitary system.

Saint-Simon's ideas continued to be advocated throughout the century as his followers went about the world building great ports, railways and canals. The most European amongst them was Charles Lemonnier who founded in 1867 the *Ligue de la Paix et de la Liberté* and published a journal under the title *Les Etats Unis d'Europe*. Auguste Comte was also much influenced by Saint-Simon. He propounded a proposal for a *Republique occidentale* consisting of five great powers (France, Germany, Italy, Spain and England) and various associate members. He envisaged its eventual extension to twelve other countries including the USA and was the first to suggest a common currency.

During the nineteenth century the European Idea for the first time gained fairly widespread acceptance, in particular in France, though in very vague and largely self-contradictory forms. Liberals, republicans, socialists and romantics dreamt of a united Europe: as men overcame their tyrants they would become freed from the artificial frontiers imposed upon them and Europe would be made. These men were patriots and nationalists too, and as such saw Europe as either a simple alliance of states or as some sort of super-state modelled upon their own particular nation. In Giuseppe Mazzini this contradiction is perhaps most clearly seen. Ardent advocate of both Italian and European unity, he never made it clear how the two were to be reconciled.

An odd combination of republicanism, socialism and romanticism is indeed typical of this period. In 1831 J.-P. Buchez founded in Paris the paper *Europeén* to propagate Christian Socialism and the idea of a Federation. Victor Considérant, in his *La Dernière Guerre et la Paix Définitive en Europe* (1850) prescribes a highly centralized European state yet maintains that it must respect the rights of nationalities. Lamennais proclaims that 'all the fractions of the human race gravitate towards one great unity'. Lamartine, in the *Marseillaise de la Paix*, writes:

'Le monde en s'éclairant s'élève à l'unité.
Je suis concitoyen de tout homme qui pense.
La Verité est mon pays.'

And later, as Minister of Foreign Affairs in 1848, he published a *Manifeste à l'Europe* announcing the eventual creation of international fraternity throughout the globe. Victor Hugo states categorically: '*A coup sûr, la République européenne, nous l'aurons.*' And in 1847, presiding at a peace conference organized in Paris by Mazzini, he declares that 'the day will come when bullets and bombs are replaced by votes, by the universal suffrage of the people, by the venerable arbitration of a sovereign senate which will be to Europe as Parliament is to England, the Diet to Germany and the legislative Assembly to France.' And in 1870, sitting in the National Assembly in Bordeaux, he even proposes fusion with the victorious Prussians: 'No more frontiers! The Rhine for all. Let us be the same republic, the United States of Europe, the Continental Federation, European liberty, universal peace!' The proclamation of the Second Republic in

1848 had indeed given a great fillip to the European Idea. Littré's sentiments are typical:

'The feeling of European fraternity increases as the revolution is propagated and the democratic cause gains new adherents. ... It is time international committees were formed to prepare people's minds for the democratic fusion that must come about. By its history, by its sentiments and by its interests, the West is pushed towards a republican Confederation.'

The one person in France of the time who saw and overcame these contradictions was the great socialist thinker, Proudhon, though not until late in his life. *Du Principe fédératif* (1863) gives the first real definition of federalism. Proudhon was the first thinker to maintain that nationalism was evil in itself, an abstraction 'the product of politics rather than of nature'. Nationalism leads inevitably to war, compromises personal liberties and reinforces the dictatorial powers of the state. But Proudhon accepts that both in terms of what is practical and of justice nationalism cannot simply be abolished. The right of people, or groups of people, to govern themselves cannot be denied, and the unitary state whether on a European or a national scale, cannot safeguard that right. Thus the states coming together in the Federation must themselves be federations so that the necessary local autonomy may be assured. Federalism is for him 'the supreme guarantee of all liberty and of all law, and must, without soldiers or priests, replace both feudal and Christian society.' But he admits that this system demands revolution, which he considers unlikely. His work in general was greatly overshadowed by that of Karl Marx, and that part dealing with international affairs went particularly unheeded. Yet today his ideas of what would now be termed 'integral federalism', naïve as they may appear, are nevertheless singularly relevant. One should not neglect the strange warning he gives to posterity in *Du Principe fédératif*: 'The twentieth century will open the era of federations, or humanity will begin again a purgatory of a thousand years.'

36

Karl Marx himself was never directly interested in European unity. He despised nationalism certainly, but the important barrier was that of class. Once this was overcome, the problem of nationalities would solve itself. He had no time for what he termed 'chimeras of a European Republic, of a perpetual peace . . .' And however internationalist he may have been in principle, his ideal society was a highly centralized one far removed from federalism. He was in some respects the absolute idealist, the Plato of the day. The possibility that one day his theories would be applied by a barbarous Russia, for which country he had nothing but contempt, would have seemed to him contrary to all reason.

Under the lengthening shadow of German Imperialism, the Tsar Nicholas II in 1898 proposed a peace conference. This took place at The Hague the following year. Despite the German representative's announcement at the beginning of the proceedings that his Government was not opposed to war *a priori*, the conference had a limited success in producing the International Court at The Hague. A second conference was held in 1907, this time on American initiative, which did useful work in codifying the rules of international law, but could do nothing to relieve the steadily mounting international tension.

An interesting gathering had also been held in Paris in 1900 at which the threat of war forced more down-to-earth and materialist minds to follow the paths trodden by earlier thinkers. One Anatole Leroy-Beaulieu, bourgeois lawyer and sociologist and a member of the Institut de France, organized the *Conférence des Sciences politiques* and in his opening address advanced new reasons for supporting European federation:

'It is no longer only the dreamers and philosophers, men in love with a perhaps superhuman ideal of peace and justice, who long to realize the old utopian idea of a European union. It is also more positive minds, concerned above all about material interests or political advantages and preoccupied with the damage which its hates and internal divisions could bring to ancient Europe. . .'

Leroy-Beaulieu put forward a plan for a European federation with the significant exclusion of England (a world, rather than a European power) and Russia (a foreign culture).

At this stage the tragic suicidal instincts of Christendom took over and the First World War began. The Peace Conference which led to the Treaty of Versailles in 1919 was a nationalistic orgy. With the exception of President Wilson all concerned were determined to extract their pound of flesh and the national frontiers of post-war Europe were the direct result of this bargaining. The American President did, however, succeed in his insistence that the fragile balance be supported by some form of international institution. Thus the League of Nations was born. Though the European countries were numerically in a slight minority, the fact that Russia was not a member and that the USA soon withdrew meant that the organization was in effect a European structure. It suffered from all those contradictions so evident in most of the plans for European union from Pierre Dubois onwards. It left national sovereignty intact; could in practice use no sanctions to enforce its decisions; and was therefore incapable of solving anything but the most minor problems. Nevertheless, for the first time in modern history an attempt had been made to regulate the relations between states by means other than force. The League of Nations was therefore a new, if unsuccessful, experiment in international relationships, and as such afforded invaluable experience. It was probably an essential first step towards a goal which we have certainly not got to yet.

As the ineffectiveness of the League of Nations became progressively more evident, thoughts again turned to the possibilities of a purely European arrangement involving some element of federalism. The best known of the early advocates of such a course is Count Richard Coudenhove-Kalergi, who published in 1923 his first book entitled *Pan-Europa*. He proposed a federal system not dissimilar to that of the USA and believed that national parliaments could be persuaded to renounce the necessary degree of sovereignty. In order to achieve this he planned to educate public opinion, and encouraged by the success of his book, founded the Pan-European Movement the following year for this purpose. This too was a great success; national sections sprang up everywhere and many public figures associated themselves with it. Various other groups also appeared about this time, notably the *Union économique et douanière européenne* in 1926 and the *Fédération pour l'Entente européenne* in 1927. The same year Louis Loucheur, the French Minister, proposed the creation of European cartels for coal, steel and wheat – foreshadowing the Schuman Plan and the former Green Plan.

The first official plea for European unity after the war was made in January 1925 by Edouard Herriot. But it was the famous 'Briand initiative' at the League of Nations in 1929 that at last forced governments to take account of the European Idea. After sounding out opinion in his own parliament and country, and among other national leaders (Gustav Stresemann, the Foreign Minister in the Weimar Republic, supported the idea; Ramsay MacDonald considered it premature; and Mussolini made it a condition of his support that all colonies became the common property of the federation), Aristide Briand, former French Foreign Minister and very recently President of the Council, announced his plan on 7 September. 'I think,' he said,

> 'that among peoples who are geographically grouped together like the peoples of Europe there must exist a sort of federal link. .... It is this link which I wish to endeavour to establish. Evidently the association will act mainly in the economic sphere. That is the most pressing question. But I am sure also that from a political point of view, and from a social point of view the federal link, without infringing the sovereignty of any of the nations which might take part in such as association, could be beneficial.'

The old contradiction is apparent. True Briand aimed at a federation and not a unitary state, but nevertheless insisted that national sovereignty should in no way be affected. Though this was undoubtedly intended in part to allay the fears of his audience, it seems that Briand had no very clear idea at all of what would or would not even be given up. Stresemann and Benes, the Czechoslovakian Minister, and a number of lesser representatives supported the proposals. Britain remained silent. Briand was requested to prepare a memorandum for the next session of the League of Nations. This was sent to the governments in May 1930. Reactions received were all favourable but vague – with the exception of the British which was not vague but unfavourable. But when the eleventh session of the League opened it became rapidly clear that the divergences of view were many and probably insuperable. A study commission was set up to prepare a complete report – and as so often happens, reference to a commission meant the end. The commission met periodically until 1932 under Briand's chairmanship, but when, in that year, he died, the commission died also.

During the ensuing years a number of people, including some very eminent ones, continued to advocate federal ideas, and a number of new bodies were set up to do the same – in particular the Europa-Union movement, created in Basle in 1933, the *Union Douanière européenne* in France in 1930, the European Parliamentary Union, and in 1938 Federal Union in Britain. All this, however, was in the shadow of the second German threat to dominate the Continent by force of arms and was therefore in the circumstances quite unrealistic.

It will be seen that for nearly seven hundred years, indeed ever since the collapse of the original European Idea, what used to be Christendom has been struggling with the problem of its own unity. We have now traced briefly the attempts to achieve this by force or, alternatively, by reason. All failed. Are we once again to see the collapse of a final experiment which can only work if the nation-state can be induced to modify its absolute pretensions? Readers, if they persevere beyond this point, will be able to make up their own minds on whether we shall once again have to drain to its dregs the urn of bitter prophecy.

CHAPTER FOUR

*

Europe Since the War

WITH this background we approach the present, and I shall seek to describe the immediate reasons for our present discontents.

Let us go back then to 1945, only twenty years ago, an instant in the eye of history, but long enough for half the nation to forget and for the other half not to be able to remember. Since Stalingrad and El Alamein at the end of 1942 the Nazis and the Fascists had been on the defensive and the tide of war had also turned in the Pacific, The Conference of Yalta (from which the French were excluded) at the beginning of the year had in effect confirmed the dubious policy of unconditional surrender and had agreed the procedure for dealing with a prostrate Germany and with 'liberated' allies – this last agreement promptly violated by Stalin in the case of the Poles. After the surrender in May there was the Conference of Potsdam (from which the French were again excluded) and the establishment of the short-lived Tripartite Government of Germany. Just previously the Western Allies, instead of using the violation by the Russians of the Yalta Declaration on liberated Europe as an excuse for keeping their armies on the line which they had reached, withdrew them into the previously agreed zones, thereby handing over Leipzig and a large part of Germany to the Russians and going a long way towards losing the peace. After only a few months it nevertheless became apparent that real co-operation with the Russians was an illusion and that the division of Germany was inevitable. The cold war began: Western Germany was organized as a separate state: the French, on British insistence, were finally brought in as an equal (it was true that they had spent a difficult year putting their own house in order) and on both sides of the Iron Curtain the clearing up process began.

At this point there was no doubt at all about who were the leaders of the Western world. They were the United States associated with Britain and her 'Commonwealth and Empire'. The Commonwealth was it is true to a large extent independent – certainly the 'White' Commonwealth was – but even among those members of it Britain was still considered a sort of *primus inter pares* whose lead they would be apt to follow as likely as not. The Empire on the other hand was a powerful instrument still capable of being used for its own high purposes by the mother country – 450 million in India, another ninety million elsewhere outside Britain, in all about a quarter of the entire population of the globe. In Britain's own estimation this complex of nations of which she was the head placed her in a special category as a Great Power, perhaps not altogether as powerful as America, but still in a category far removed from states such as France or Italy, even if – as the phrase always went at the time – the former 'recovered her greatness', whatever that might mean.

So the idea that a power of Britain's size would ever enter some European Union as an equal would hardly have occurred to any representative British subject in 1945. Associating with our neighbours on some basis of unanimity was one thing: union entirely another. Still less would it have seemed possible to unite with our former enemies, recently defeated in a long and desperate struggle. We were, in our own opinion and largely rightly, one of the three victor powers. It was again on our insistence that, at long last, France was finally admitted to that category, for most people then believed that France, far from being our equal, had for historical and tactical reasons only been created (along with Nationalist China) a Permanent Member of the Security Council of the United Nations. We on the other hand were a real world power; we had, owing to the comradeship of the war and the language, a 'special relationship' with the United States; we had, if not yet a bomb, at least the nuclear know-how. British troops were in Egypt, Libya, Greece, Iraq and Transjordan; the great Indian Army was at our command; we had huge bases at Gibraltar, Malta, the Canal Zone, Aden and Singapore; the King's African Rifles were a force in Africa; our Navy was the second and our Air Force the third largest in the world; even the Boers had fought on our side in North Africa. The general British contribution to victory had by any standard been immense. It might well have been thought that the British Commonwealth and Empire had reached its splendid apogee. And yet, within about fifteen years, almost all this had disappeared. Why?

The fact was, we were much more exhausted by our death struggle than we knew. The abrupt ending of Lend Lease in 1945 had shown up the extent of our economic weakness and the drain on our reserves that we had been obliged to make in order to keep ourselves alive. Our very victory too had been in some ways a disadvantage in that it did not compel us to reconstruct our factories, write off our debt, work like beavers and start again (as the Germans did) from scratch. The old habits therefore persisted. We tended to think that we had done so well – as we had – in the war that the world more or less owed us a living. This particular feeling was enhanced by the mere existence of the Commonwealth and Empire, which Mr Churchill said he had not been appointed the King's First Minister to liquidate.

Yet this is what we had to do. If for no better reason than that of making a virtue of necessity, the third Labour Government of 1945 embarked, as one of their first tasks, on the 'liberation' of India. Once this had been accomplished – brutally and unsatisfactorily but still accomplished – the flood gates were opened. Complete independence for every heretofore dependent state in the Empire was the only solution. Today it is to all intents and purposes a fact, and it is useless to comfort ourselves with the illusion that this process has in some way strengthened the country. Inevitable, even desirable the process may have been; but its inherent cause was not the goodwill – it was indeed immense – but the weakness of the metropolis. The loss of Empire may indeed have had certain positive economic advantages, provided always that we are not drawn into expensive wars to defend what we have lost already. But politically it must surely be obvious to all that we are much less powerful than we were before.

In 1945, however, all this was for the future. Then, and right up till 1950 or so, when this country together with strong contingents from the Commonwealth played a notable part in the Korean War as the major ally of the United States, it was entirely possible to assume that we were, as a state, in a completely different category from France, to say nothing of Germany, Italy or indeed Japan. It needed Suez and repeated economic crises to demonstrate that our famous 'special and separate position' was no longer tenable, and this in spite of the fact that we had, in the interval, exploded our own hydrogen bomb and entered the atomic club, of which in a sense, of course, we were already a founder member. Thus when in the West's relationship with the Soviet Union the show-down had come with the '*coup de Prague*' of 1948, and, subsequently, with the Berlin blockade, it was still Britain who was the principal support and counsellor of the United States. Similarly when in 1947 it was a case of saving Western Europe from collapse by economic means, it was Britain who, under the genial impulse of Ernest Bevin, took the lead in distributing Marshall Aid and in founding the Organization of European Economic Co-operation in Paris. As permanent president of that excellent institution, Britain also took the lead in demobilizing all physical restrictions on inter-European trade, notably quotas, and in founding the European Payments Union, thus laying the essential foundations for any European co-operation. But all this was done on the quiet assumption that there was a difference in status between us and the other European States involved. Our basic theory of that time, was, of course that the UK lay within three over-lapping circles – the Commonwealth, America and Europe. Of the first we were the centre, all united in the person of HM The Queen. The second revolved round our alleged 'special relationship' with the United States. The third was largely a geographical consideration, given the obvious fact that we were from this point of view part of Europe and had been mixed up with its peoples in one way or another for several thousands of years.

It was, however, in 1948 when the great debate began on the political, as opposed to the economic, reconstruction of Europe that Britain's national attitude of separateness and indeed superiority became absolutely clear. Here our basic governmental contention was that we would agree to anything on one condition, namely, that there was no element of 'supranationalism' which might conceivably result in our one day being merged in a greater whole. It was for this reason that we rejected the original idea that the OEEC might be a Customs Union. Likewise, when it came to discussions on the Council of Europe, we successfully insisted on unanimity for decisions in the Council of Ministers and we repudiated any suggestion that this Council should be dependent on an elected or even on a non-elected parliament. This attitude in the light of hindsight may be thought to be unfortunate: it was, however, almost inevitable in the circumstances. Certainly no British Government at that time could have accepted the supra-national principle even in an attenuated form. To have done so would have meant repudiation by the House of Commons and the nation.

Britain went further, however: when the Statute of the Council of Europe was negotiated in 1948, she saw to it that not only was it a mere shadow of a union, but that it even laid down that the Council should have nothing whatever to do with defence. To be frank, Mr Bevin did not really believe in any kind of European Idea. If anything he was against it. Some form of Atlantic Union based on Anglo-American leadership he could understand. It made sense to him; and as soon as he could after the conclusion of the Brussels Treaty he sent me off to America in great secrecy to negotiate in the recesses of the Pentagon what eventually turned out to be the North Atlantic Treaty.

Indeed our original draft was not changed very much. Nor can there be any doubt that at that moment of time (early 1948) with the Russians clearly challenging the entire West it was much more important than efforts to unite Western Europe only. Mr Bevin's priorities were entirely right, but his basic instinct, I feel, was wrong if only because he did not appreciate the strong urge towards real European unity and the likely consequences for Britain if this were by any chance successful. Let us now examine the progress of what I may suitably call the counter-thesis, namely, the general notion that European unity is desirable and only achievable on the basis of some kind of supra-nationality.

All through this initial post-war period the voice of the European Unionists – sometimes called Federalists, but in any case those in favour of an organic as opposed to a confederal organization of Europe – had been gathering strength. And this was only natural. As opposed to Britain, all the states of geographical Europe from Nizhny-Novgorod to Seville, with the small exceptions of Sweden, Switzerland and Portugal (Spain could be counted in this category too because of her appalling civil war) had between 1939 and 1945 been defeated, bombarded, pillaged, 'liberated' and generally rolled in the mud. Their institutions had been suppressed, many of their subjects thrown into prison, murdered or carried off into slavery. All, I repeat, whether officially conquerors or conquered, had undergone this terrible experience. It was perhaps not unnatural in the circumstances that the more intelligent in these countries should begin to nurse heretical doubts about the continuing validity, the sacrosanctity, of the famous nation-state.

At the end of 1945 there arrived back in France a haggard band of living skeletons in striped uniforms known as *les deportés*. They were the survivors of the appalling German concentration camps. Many of these had had every opportunity of reflecting on the nature of the political set-up that they would wish to see established after the war. So had, in their hide-outs, many of the most remarkable of the *résistants* who had escaped the attentions of the Gestapo. These men, and others, had reached the conclusion that the only sure way to prevent a repetition of the horrors which they had endured was to form some European union which was something more than the sum of its component parts; in other words an entity with a personality of its own which would limit the complete freedom of action of the individual nation-state. At the same time most of them believed that the last thing they wanted was the creation of a huge soulless bureaucracy that might, no one could say, be run one day on totalitarian lines. They were therefore most keen on a parliamentary element and some of them were pre-pared to say that from the start any European executive that might be created would in some way be dependent on a directly elected European Assembly. These 'Federalists' as they came to be known were in the beginning largely French, but they were soon joined by others from the Low Countries, Germany and Italy who for the most part had been courageous opponents of the Nazi or Fascist régimes. The various Federalist move-ments, to which might be added Count Coudenhove-Kalergi's separate 'Pan-Europa' organization, all played a notable part in pushing the counter-thesis, but often they undermined their own influence by supporting extreme solutions which involved the effective suppression of the various nations.

In 1946, however, Mr Churchill himself made a great speech at Zurich, in which he urged a coming together of France and her secular enemy Germany and spoke of the United States of Europe of which Great Britain and the Commonwealth, 'mighty America', and perhaps even the USSR would be the 'sponsors and guardians'. The following year, after two years in opposition, he presided over the famous European Conference of The Hague. The European Movement was there established. Its other leaders were Leon Blum, Alcide de Gasperi and Paul Henri Spaak (Konrad Adenauer was to join much later). In the background – though not at The Hague – was Monsieur Jean Monnet, who had worked with the Allies on economic planning in Washington during the war. A number of distinguished politicians, such as Monsieur Guy Mollet, Monsieur Paul

Reynaud and Mr Macmillan were associated with these leaders. The Chairman of the Executive Committee was Mr Duncan Sandys. Of the British nearly all were drawn from the ranks of the Conservatives, who were then in opposition and able to express their sentiments more freely, but there were a few excellent Labour representatives as well.

The recommendations of the Conference undoubtedly had an effect on events, as did the later pronouncements of the Movement. The Governments were induced to set up an official committee to consider the whole problem of European unity. I myself was deputy to Mr Dalton on this committee which also included Lord Bridges and the late Lord Inverchapel. On the political side we had before us the Political Report of the Congress which said that 'if therefore the policy of mutual aid, . . . is to bear any substantial fruit, it must be accompanied step by step with a parallel policy of closer political union. *Sooner or later this must involve the renunciation of, or to be more accurate, the joint exercise of certain sovereign powers.*'

There was, however, an uncertainty behind the Hague declarations. It was never clear, in fact, how far, if at all, Mr Churchill associated himself with the Federal thesis at any rate so far as Britain was concerned. Resounding phrases in favour of European unity were one thing: definite assurances that Britain would be prepared to accept even a small element of supranationality was quite another. What was entirely clear was that the British Government of the day, for its part, was absolutely opposed to anything of the kind. Many of the recommendations of The Hague Conference were in fact accepted by the governments, including that for a Consultative Assembly. As we have seen, the Council of Europe was indeed established, but only on condition that it had no effective power.

Nevertheless the idea of a European Defence Community – which was strongly reinforced by proposals for a 'European Army' in 1950 – persisted after the constitution of the Council of Europe in 1949, and the final project known as the 'Pleven Plan' involving the actual integration of a European force right down to battalion level was, under the impulse of the Korean War, prepared, mostly on French initiative, and actually signed in 1952. There was provision for a European Parliament with special powers and great enthusiasm for the idea was engendered in the countries of what are now the Six. For it was generally assumed that only by the adoption of some similar device could the French be induced to agree to the rearmament of the Germans. It was also assumed that even if Britain could not join the European Defence Community she would nevertheless in some way be closely associated with it. It was finally assumed that when and if Mr Churchill and the Conservatives returned to power, they would be at any rate far more favourably disposed to participation in the project than the Labour Government.

When he came back to power, however, in 1951, Mr Churchill made it quite clear that this was not so. Mr Eden made a speech in Rome while the Council of Europe was actually in session in which he said that Britain could have nothing to do with the European Army; we wished it well but could not join it ourselves. This blunt effort shattered all illusions, even those apparently entertained by the British chief representative in the Council of Europe Assembly, Sir David Maxwell Fyfe (as he then was), who came out with a rather different announcement. Monsieur Spaak, the very pro-British President of the Council of Europe Assembly, resigned. There was a general feeling that Britain had nowhere near reached the stage at which she contemplated any really meaningful association with her closest neighbours. All that was only thirteen years ago. Eventually the European Defence Community was, it is true, repudiated by its parent France, the French National Assembly failing to vote the necessary legislation by a fairly large majority in August 1954. This was the nadir of the hopes of the continental 'Europeans', and it may also be that this reverse was to a considerable extent due to the non-cooperative attitude of the British Government. In any case, the 'Europeans' drew the necessary conclusion that it was too soon to think of unifying Europe by direct political means involving the delicate subject of defence, and that it would be preferable to try to achieve the end in the first instance by economic action.

They had already had a notable success in this field. In May 1950 Monsieur Schuman proposed a scheme for a Coal and Steel Authority which would put the coal and steel industries of Western Europe under common direction, and, in the last resort solve problems of rationalization and redundancy by means of a supra-national 'High Authority' placed under the broad control of a special European Assembly. This project, the author of which was of course Monsieur Jean Monnet, met with instant hostility on the part of the Labour Government who had already made it clear that they would have nothing whatever to do with the European Army either. Nevertheless the project went ahead and was signed in April 1951. It has proved to be a great success and there seems now to be general regret that Britain could not go along with it. Had she done so, it seems likely not only that our coal and steel industries would have benefited but, much more important, Britain would have been set in the direction of some kind of economic union with Western Europe which after the reverse of the European Defence Community in 1950 became, as we have seen, the next objective of the European Federalists. We can therefore legitimately say that in spite of Mr Eden's successful efforts to set up some kind of defensive organization in Western Europe which had followed the breakdown of a project for a European Army, Britain, by the end of 1954, had missed two major opportunities for coming together in any real sense with her European neighbours: the first was her repudiation of the Coal and Steel Community: the second was her uncooperative attitude towards the European Defence Community.

It is true that in the Western European Union which was established early in 1955 chiefly in order to legalize the rearmament of the Germans in the face of a continuing Soviet menace, Her Majesty's Government for the first time agreed to a very small supra-national element, namely, not to reduce her forces in Germany except with the consent of the Council of Ministers. But this was hedged round with various conditions which detracted a good deal from its positive value. Otherwise, the Western European Union was in entire accordance with the well-known British philosophy which had consistently prevailed (except in the case of the Coal and Steel Community) owing to the efforts of successive governments since 1945. It looked indeed at this point as if this theory had finally triumphed and that what one might call the counter-thesis was virtually dead. However, as a result of continuous work behind the scenes by Monsieur Monnet and his friends, there took place in March 1955 the historic Conference of Messina. Foiled on the political front the Europeans decided to revert to that of economic. The agenda at Messina was no less a thing than a European Economic Union. Britain was of course invited to participate in the subsequent Spaak Committee but only sent an official of the Board of Trade who was withdrawn after a few weeks. The fact was that, as usual, the British Government was opposed in principle to the objectives which the Six were now setting before themselves. It was obvious that if the objective was only a simple customs union Britain could not join except by sacrificing something of her own guiding principle of complete national independence tempered only by co-operation with institutions governed by the working of the unanimity rule. It was also a fact that the British Government just did not believe that the Six could agree even on a customs union. Had not Benelux, the customs union of the three component parts of the Low Countries been a partial failure? How could agreement possibly be reached when it came, for instance, to exposing French and Italian industry to the rigours of German competition? The proposals did not seem to the British to make any real sense.

We underestimated the force of the European Idea. Not only was the objective defined as something beyond a mere customs union but actually an economic union and (implicitly) an eventual political union as well, and as a result of intensive work in a committee presided over by Monsieur Spaak a treaty was actually signed in Rome on 25 March 1957 and came into force, after ratification by all the parliaments concerned on 1

January 1958. Worse still from our point of view, it did not contain any of the features which might have modified it had the British taken part in the negotiations. In particular, as we now know to our cost, an article provided that new members could only join if there was unanimity in the Council of Ministers, in other words it embodied the famous veto. It was evident in the light of hindsight that the withdrawal of Mr Bretherton from the Spaak Committee was the third and indeed the most significant of Britain's missed opportunities for coming to grips with the European problem. It must be admitted that the final success of the 'Europeans' was facilitated by an event that occurred at the end of 1956 and seemed to prove to the continentals that Britain was no longer in such a special and indeed superior position as she had appeared to be up till then. The Suez adventure conclusively demonstrated to the French, at any rate, that there was no possibility of any independent European foreign policy unless Europeans came together in some wider entity. Moreover, Suez undoubtedly resulted in a general recovery of self-confidence by the French nation. Though the expedition had been a total failure the French Army had done just as well from the military point of view as the British. Some might even allege that they had done rather better. Though France had failed to secure her objective so after all had Britain for whom failure obviously had far wider and more far-reaching consequences.

Conscious therefore now of the dangers involved, the British Government strove by all the means in their power to push alternative means for unifying Western Europe economically, more particularly the idea of a European Free Trade Area. This had many advantages from our point of view and that of certain other European countries. It might even have had distinct advantages from the point of view of one or two members of the Six. A single market (with exceptions), though no common tariff, would undoubtedly have been created thereby, but since agriculture was excluded it is clear that there would have been few compensations for at any rate the Italians and the French. Moreover, its object was totally dissimilar. There was no question of setting up any kind of economic union – indeed there could not be if the unanimity principle were to be preserved – still less was there any hint of any eventual political or defence machinery. Small wonder indeed, again in the light of hindsight, that the French refused to adopt this plan in the OEEC at the end of 1958, which meant in effect that the Six would continue in their independent economic way without the participation of Britain. Britain's subsequent action in forming the Free Trade Area among those European states which could not or would not contemplate joining the European Economic Community was understandable enough, not only as a bargaining gesture, but also as an effort to increase her home market substantially in the event of her never being able to get into the Community. But it did not have the political appeal of the latter and it seemed at least doubtful even then whether, supposing the community achieved the status of a real economic union, it could maintain itself as an entity unless it adopted some of the techniques embodied in the Treaty of Rome.

For two and a half years the British Government considered its position and took stock of the advantages and disadvantages of actually joining the EEC. During his successful state visit to London in May 1960, General de Gaulle is supposed to have given some encouragement to the idea that the United Kingdom might one day join the Six. Indeed I myself had the impression that he would not be opposed to this in certain circumstances. Where there might well have been some misunderstanding, however, lay in the nature of the circumstances which General de Gaulle probably had in mind. Late in 1960 the Western European Union Assembly, under the influence of Mr Peter Kirk and other prominent British 'Europeans' passed a resolution urging the British Government to apply for membership of the EEC, and in the late spring of the following year I presided over the Common Market Campaign in the United Kingdom. This produced a document signed by 150 prominent persons of all walks and parties (see Appendix 1) which set out the case for our taking the plunge and applying for membership, thereafter negotiating on the three outstanding problems, namely, British agriculture, Commonwealth trade, and the interests of our EFTA colleagues. Gradually the British press came round for the most part to this idea.

At the end of July 1961 the British Government finally made up its mind that it wanted to join the Community and put in its necessary application to the Commission in Brussels in accordance with the Treaty. If anything was clear it was that this decision represented a complete revolution in British political thinking. The Treaty of Rome embodies a number of supranational features the most significant of which is the necessity (especially in the third phase) of taking decisions in certain fields by qualified majority vote. It also confers a definite and in some respects an entirely independent rôle on the Commission in Brussels. Finally, it provides ultimately for a directly elected European Parliament on which to some extent the Commission depends. Only eleven years previously the British Government had refused to have anything to do with the much less far reaching Coal and Steel Authority on the grounds that it embodied some rather similar supra-national features. Only ten years before they had made it clear that, for much the same reason, they would equally have nothing to do with the European Army. Only six years before they had declined even to participate in the negotiations for the Common Market. Now they put aside all these objections and came out flatly for a supranational solution. Few people across the Channel, few perhaps in Britain itself, realized the magnitude of the change in British policy which had been accomplished. Virtually it meant that in the face of a potential menace exerted by a super-power which had already occupied a great part of Eastern Europe, the British Government were abandoning the policy of European balance which they had successfully pursued for something like four hundred years.

It is not, however, clear that even all members of the British Government itself, though some may have been undoubtedly conscious of the historic importance of the application, were alive to its real significance. For understandable political reasons the Government did little or nothing to enlighten the public about the real nature of the application. It is true that on one occasion in April 1962 during the progress of the abortive negotiations Mr Heath did go so far as to say that Britain accepted all the economic *and political* implications of the Treaty of Rome, but this undertaking was not echoed by his colleagues, thereby in the first place giving rise to some suspicions on the part of the 'Europeans' that we were not altogether sincere in our desire to join an eventual European Political Community and, in the second place, to allegations on the part of the anti-Common Marketeers that there was on foot a sinister plot to destroy all vestiges of British independence. It seems likely that an earlier effort to enlighten the British public on what exactly the political implications of the Treaty were would have had an excellent effect and might conceivably have produced a situation in which Britain could at an earlier stage have made proposals which it would have been very difficult even for the French Government not to have accepted. So would some suggestion that British acceptance of the principle of supra-nationality, though epoch making, could not result, for reasons that might have been given, in any suppression of the individuality or personality of Britain itself. Assuming the continuance of the EEC such a failure though, as I say, politically comprehensible, represents the fourth of Britain's great missed opportunities.

Now it is conceivable that the great attempt to limit by general agreement the total independence of the European nation-state may yet fail or, at the least, fail to make further progress. Those who believe with President de Gaulle that such an effort is contrary to nature – and there are still many in Britain who do believe this also – may yet be proved right. It is entirely possible to argue that it was for the very reason that had we come into the EEC we would have used our influence in favour of making it work in accordance with the Treaty of Rome that General de Gaulle exercised his veto. He may, as he hinted in 1960, have been prepared to welcome our eventual entry into Europe, but only on condition that it was a Europe fashioned in accordance with his own national ideas and not any kind of supra-national entity. In the light of such considerations, it does not seem to matter very much whether there was or was not a real misunderstanding between the General and Mr Macmillan at the famous conference of Rambouillet in December 1962. It is, I repeat, true that had we come up with our own ideas for what the desirable features of any European Political and Defence Community might be we might have made it more difficult, more particularly before the French elections, for the General to veto our application, especially if these proposals had embodied the feature of real co-operation between the two European *Forces de Frappe*. But the fundamental issue, and this now applies to Western Europe as a whole, is between those who believe in the emergence of some union which is more than a mere alliance and those who believe that we shall all sooner rather than later revert to a collection of totally independent small and medium states who will, whatever their professions, increasingly come under the influence of one super-power or the other. How, then, does the European Economic Community actually work?

CHAPTER FIVE

*

How the Community Works

THE first thing to grasp about the European Economic Community is that, politically speaking, it is based on an entirely new and original idea. Internationally nothing like it has ever been tried out before. We have of course had customs unions and they have usually given birth to some kind of political union in which the component parts are just merged in some greater whole – for example, in the way the state members of the famous German Zollverein under Prussian pressure were eventually incorporated in the new German Empire. But the EEC, on the contrary, has established a definite economic machine which, if suitably operated, can blossom out into a political structure in which, though they cannot obviously have complete freedom of action, there is no reason to suppose that the component states will lose their individuality or their personality. That is its essential originality and attraction. Whether it will indeed blossom out still remains to be seen. But it has already advanced far enough to show that the whole conception is entirely feasible and that it is the only practicable way of coping with the problem of exaggerated and out-dated nationalism.

The chief feature of the EEC is of course the Council of Ministers which, unless the Treaty of Rome is violated or modified by agreement, will operate in many important sectors by means of a qualified majority vote once the Community has entered into the third and final three-year stage of its transitional period. The formula governing this is most ingeniously constructed to suit the needs of the Six themselves, and to those of us

57

accustomed to the traditional parliamentary method of taking decisions it may seem rather complicated. On a number of very minor matters a simple majority will suffice but the more important issues can be decided only by a 'qualified' majority of twelve votes out of seventeen. The three larger countries have four votes each, Belgium and the Netherlands two each, and Luxembourg one. When a vote is taken on a proposal coming up from the Commission, twelve votes can carry it. It will therefore be seen that when the Commission has given its approval to any plan, the three larger powers can, if necessary, push it through against the wishes of the smaller powers, and that equally one of the larger powers can block a proposal provided only that it is supported by either Belgium or the Netherlands. On the other hand, any other issue must be decided by twelve votes in favour 'cast by at least four members'. It will be observed therefore that if a proposal has not already had the approval of the Commission it is not possible for the three larger powers to railroad it through and that at any rate one of the smaller powers must express consent also.

A feature which is anathema to General de Gaulle and the French nationalists is of course the possibility that once a system of majority voting has come into force one of the larger powers, and notably France, could be placed in a minority of one and a decision taken over France's head. This is nevertheless an essential feature of the Treaty to which France solemnly put her signature in 1957 and which was subsequently ratified by the French Parliament. If the French nation should now go back on this vital provision of the Treaty, it would rightly be regarded as a great betrayal of the European Idea. It might be added that it is quite unlikely that any serious decision will be taken over the dead body of any major European power since (a) the whole issue will already have been fought out in an independent Commission and (b) unless the recalcitrant large power is absolutely unreasonable, it is likely that it would receive the support of at any rate one of the smaller powers. All these things will in practice be worked out by a process of continuous discussion, and if agreement really cannot be reached it is more likely that the issue will be postponed rather than that a big stick will be applied to the large power by all the other members of the group. Nevertheless the existence of this big stick in the cupboard is something which must be accepted by all members of the Community if the Community is going to take on any kind of independent existence and not simply be a collection of entirely separate nation states. Finally, it may be said that even when the Common Market is fully operative unanimity will still be required on certain fundamental matters including, for example, the admission of a new member state. This was the essential point made in my recent correspondence with Count Coudenhove-Kalergi, which is reproduced in Appendix 3.

The other essential and indeed the really novel feature of the Community is the Commission. This consists of nine members 'chosen for their general competence and of indisputable independence' by the Ministers acting in unanimity, and is entrusted with the general duty of 'ensuring the functioning and development of the Common Market'. In doing so it has very considerable independent powers; for instance, if it feels that any part of the Treaty is being infringed by a member state, it can take that member to the European Court. It is thus much more than a mere executive body. It has important powers of initiative as well, and can put up recommendations on any matter dealt with by the Treaty whenever it considers necessary. It can therefore be said that it is both the conscience and the operative machine of the Community. Moreover, in principle, and even now in practice, it actually does undertake international commercial negotiations on behalf of the Community as a whole. Finally it is clear that when agreement is reached on how much of the vast sums accruing from the levies on imports of foodstuffs are to be paid into a central fund the Commission will have a great say in their disposal. If it should be decided that customs dues should likewise be paid into such a central fund (as is provisionally authorized under Article 201 of the Treaty), it seems probable that the Commission will within a few years have the dominant say in the disposal of a sum approaching £1,000 million a year.

It is true that its recommendations as regards the development of the Treaty (for example, the preparation of a common agricultural or transport policy) are submitted to the Council and cannot be put into force until the Council has agreed to them by the appropriate majority. But the Council can only approve or reject the Commission's proposals. It can amend them only if unanimous and on the most difficult problems this is obviously unlikely. And in many cases it is forbidden by the Treaty from acting other than upon the proposal of the Commission. Within the framework of the Treaty itself, or of regulations subsequently adopted by the Council, the Commission can issue regulations which have general application and are binding on all member states, and 'directives' which equally bind any member to which they are addressed. Both of these have to be enforced by domestic agencies. It will be seen that for its successful operation the Commission must consist of genuinely independent persons who are prepared to examine vital matters concerning all the members of the Community from a European as opposed to a purely national point of view (no more than two members of the Commission of nine can have the same nationality). But equally they must be acceptable to the governments, and there is provision in the Treaty for the Council in certain circumstances to suspend a member of the Commission or for the Court to do likewise. The European Parliament also has the right to censure the Commission and if this is done by a two-thirds majority, all members of the Commission must at once resign. Generally speaking, then, it will be seen that the Commission does have certain powers and can take certain initiatives in certain well-defined fields by itself, but on all major matters of policy it must work in partnership with the Council of Ministers, which in its turn must act in certain circumstances by qualified majority vote. The issues on which such a majority vote can be taken are all listed in the Treaty, and this system (already operating in one or two instances) comes automatically into force on 1 January 1966.

The European Parliament has only limited powers under the Treaty and is principally designed for discussion. Its opinion must be sought (but not necessarily heeded) by the Council on all important matters. It is, however, laid down in the Treaty that the members of the Parliament should eventually be directly elected by universal suffrage 'in accordance with a uniform procedure in all member states'. However, until the Council acting unanimously decides on this procedure there will be no direct elections. Until this occurs, and its powers are extended, it is evident that the Parliament will not be of great political importance. But unless the Community when formed is going to be a sort of super bureaucracy the Parliament will have to have one day an important and even eventually a decisive rôle. The fourth major institution is the European Court of Justice, consisting of seven judges and two Advocates-General. This is the final arbiter in all matters concerning the interpretation of the Treaty or of the regulations adopted by the Council in order to give effect to the Treaty.

Finally there are a number of institutions of lesser importance. The Economic and Social Council has an advisory rôle similar to that of the Parliament in the decision making process, and represents employers, trade unions, consumers and other organized groups. The European Investment Bank provides funds for investment in the lesser developed areas of the Community – notably southern Italy. The European Social Fund makes available money to help overcome any social disruption which may occur as a direct result of the implementation of the Treaty. And the Overseas Development Fund channels financial assistance to the non-European underdeveloped countries associated with the EEC. All these bodies are established under the Treaty itself, and the last two are administered by the Commission. Also administered by the Commission, but established by decision of the Council as part of the machinery of the common agricultural policy is the European Agricultural Guidance and Guarantee Fund which provides finance for subsidies to the Community's farmers and export rebates on farm produce.

The institutions of the EEC are roughly paralleled in the two other Communities, Coal and Steel and Euratom. Indeed the

Parliament, Council and Court are common to all three, and the Economic and Social Committee to the EEC and Euratom (the ECSC has a similar body called Consultative Committee). But it should also be noted that the High Authority of the ECSC and in some respects the Euratom Commission, have actually considerably more independent powers than the EEC Commission, though these are of lesser significance since their field is so restricted.

By and large the machinery of the EEC has in the past functioned well. Progress towards the establishment of a complete customs union has been far more rapid than contemplated and, unless the whole process is interrupted by French nationalism, it now seems likely that it will be completed by mid-1967, two and a half years early. Though this has been made possible largely because of continuing economic expansion in the Six, the part played by the Commission should not be underestimated. It is true that the various stages in the completion of the customs union for industrial goods are spelt out in detail in the Treaty and thus follow more or less automatically. Nevertheless, upon the initiative of the Commission the whole timetable for abolishing internal customs duties and adopting a common external tariff has been greatly accelerated. It is, however, in agriculture that the significance of the Commission's rôle can best be seen. The Treaty of Rome requires that common and harmonized policies be adopted in various fields, including that of agriculture. Yet it does not specify how, nor what these common policies shall be. It is left to the Commission to make proposals to the Council of Ministers, and after January 1966 they can be decided by a qualified majority vote. In doing this the Commission has shown that it is in fact essentially a political body. We all know from our own national experience the passions to which farming gives rise. Even in this country where only about four per cent of the population is on the land it is difficult for any government to ignore the farmers today. Because the farmer throughout Europe is highly protected and the methods of protection used in the various countries differ greatly, the problems of creating a common agricultural policy were from the outset daunting. But in effect the common policy as it is now clearly emerging follows remarkably closely the lines first set out by the Commission as early as 1959. How has the Commission been able to bring this about despite the many differences?

The basic principles of harmonized prices throughout the Community and of protection from outside by a system of variable levies were accepted relatively easily at the end of 1960; and in the marathon session which ended on 14 January 1962, detailed regulations were agreed for cereals and a number of other products. Under the cereals regulation prices were to be harmonized progressively over a transitional period from 1963–7. During this time upper and lower limits would be set. In practice harmonization meant lowering the high prices in Germany, Italy and Luxembourg, and raising the lower ones in France and the Netherlands. In fact, owing mainly to the German refusal to lower the prices their farmers would receive, when 1963 was reached there was no sign of progress. So the Commission exercised its right of initiative and proposed an entirely new formula for the single stage alignment of all grain prices at the Community average – the so-called Mansholt Plan. This was finally, though not without great difficulty, adopted at the usual marathon session in December 1964, and, like all the farm policy decisions, as part of a package deal.

This combination of marathon session and package deal became the standard method by which the Community dealt with its most difficult decisions. The form at the marathon Council meetings was for the Ministers to discuss the Commission's original proposals usually until the early hours of the morning, each stating in turn his position and the concessions he was prepared to make. At some stage, while the Ministers retired for a few hours' sleep, the Commission (which attends all Council meetings) went off to prepare new proposals in the form of a package deal designed to reconcile the national positions. This new proposal was then submitted immediately to the Council. The conclusion of the package deal makes it possible for each country to concede much more than would be politically possible in an attempt at agreement over a single item where no reciprocal concessions could be expected from its partners. Thus Italian approval over grain prices was obtained by including in the package decisions on fruit and vegetables of great importance to Italy.

It should also be added that the process was made easier by the fact that the Council (consisting of Foreign Ministers, Finance Ministers or Agricultural Ministers according to the topic in question, and sometimes of all three) meets regularly at least once a month. Its members have thus over a period of time got to know each other and each other's ways of thinking. Also they know that they cannot just agree to disagree since the matter will be on their agenda again next month and the month after. Thus the atmosphere is in many ways more akin to that of a Cabinet meeting than to that found in an international conference.

Such was the system which worked until the great row between France and her partners over agricultural policy which flared up at the end of June 1965. In general it had worked fairly well till then. On the other hand it must be remembered that decisions on farm policy were possible also because France, the most reluctant member of the Community and therefore the one with the greatest power to blackmail, saw the achievement of the Common Market for agricultural produce as essentially in her interests. Progress towards the other common policies has been slow and painful, and the new mechanism is likely to undergo its most strenuous tests yet over the next year or so. So far the French, though in many ways the odd man out in the Six, have always been able to quote the letter of the Treaty, if not the spirit, as their justification. Consequently they have had the support of the Commission, the guardian of the Treaty. This was certainly the case in the cereal price crisis. Yet in the case of the next major obstacle to be overcome – the adoption of the financial regulation without which the common farm policy is meaningless – the positions are reversed. Here the Commission and the Five were in agreement. The Rome Treaty foresees that income from the agricultural levies should go to a central Community fund and not to national exchequers. Why should the Dutch claim the levies on goods entering the Community through Rotterdam when most of them are in fact destined for Germany? As we have already seen this central fund would dispose of enormous sums of money and would increase the Commission's influence very considerably. In view of this the Dutch demanded that this money be made subject to the democratic control of the European Parliament, since it would not fall within the province of any national parliament. The Commission supported this proposal, as did all the member states except France, which, as one would expect with its present leadership, refused to contemplate any possibility of an increase in the Parliament's powers. The Commission deliberately challenged the French over this. It also proposed that, as well as the agricultural levies, industrial tariffs too should go into the central pool. The Treaty does not explicitly provide for this, yet the logic of the proposal is obvious – even if not to national Treasuries which would lose a substantial part of their revenue. At the moment of writing the impasse is total yet it must be overcome unless the Six are prepared to contemplate the breakdown of the entire system and a relapse into nationalistic anarchy.

For the first time the French were able to call upon the support of neither the Commission nor the Treaty in their support. It is in practice most unlikely that the Community will be able to force them to yield as completely as the Germans did on grain prices, and in the face of its most difficult test yet will have probably to postpone a real decision for some time. In other words, new and ingenious as the machinery is – and undoubtedly far more effective than any other known method of international collective decision-making, short of the use of force – it is still true that the Community is not yet sufficiently strong to stand up to really determined opposition from one of its principal members. Equally, however, though General de Gaulle can undoubtedly prevent further advance, it is pretty certain that the Community has by now so enmeshed the national interests of its members as to prevent him from being able to undo what has already been done, in other words to break up the existing system.

The other significant step which is now looked forward to is the fusion of the three Communities (EEC, Coal and Steel, and Euratom) into one. In February 1964 the Council of Ministers agreed that this should come about by the end of 1966 and be preceded at the end of 1964 by the merger of the three Executives. This was seen not only as a step towards rationalization but also as a political move to strengthen the Community's central authorities, since a single Executive responsible for the whole range of economic policy of the Six would obviously be psychologically and politically more influential if not legally stronger. Nevertheless the rewriting of the Treaties (necessary for the complete fusion though not just for the merger of the Executives) was probably seen by the French as an opportunity for curtailing the supra-national powers of the ECSC High Authority. On the other hand, it is highly significant that the task of redrafting a single Treaty has been given to the new single Executive and not to the states members. The merger of the Executives did not take place at the end of 1964 though not for the reasons one might have expected. No decision has ever been taken on where the Community's capital is to be. The seats of the various Community institutions, in Brussels, Luxembourg and Strasbourg, are all provisional. Yet it is inconceivable that the future capital should be elsewhere than Brussels, and therefore logical that the single Executive should straightaway install itself there. Yet Luxembourg, the present home of the ECSC, refused to allow the High Authority to leave without some suitable *quid pro quo* in both political and financial terms. The Communities then made a gesture in this direction by agreeing that certain agencies should remain in or move to Luxembourg, and it was settled that the new Executive should come into being on 1 January 1966, just one year late. Whether this will actually happen is now open to doubt, and as a consequence of this it is certain that the complete fusion of the Communities will also take longer than planned.

The Treaty of Rome is about economics. Nevertheless it is a

political document. Indeed the conclusion of any international treaty implies a political act by the signatory countries, and this is particularly true of the Common Market Treaty. If its aim is economic (the nearest thing to a mention of politics is the reference in the preamble to 'an ever closer union of the peoples of Europe'), that of its authors was essentially political: the eventual establishment of a European Community for foreign policy and defence as well as economics and eventually a true political union of Europe. Since 1958 several attempts have been made to move in that direction but have all come to nothing on account of the clash between the French view of both the structure of this new Europe and its world rôle, and those of France's partners. General de Gaulle has always insisted upon the absolute inviolability of the historic nation state; yet he accepts, if reluctantly, that if France is to be a power of world significance, she can only do this as the leader of a European Community. He has therefore urged the acceptance by the other five of a European political union for foreign policy, economics and cultural affairs, but based upon inter-governmental co-operation. The Five, and in particular the smaller countries, have rightly seen the result of such a union as the inevitable subordination of their interests to those of France, and the watering down of the limited supra-national elements in the present economic treaties. They have therefore insisted upon the inclusion in the treaty of political union of at least a degree of supra-nationalism (in fact the extension to the political field of the so-called Community method) and the exclusion of all reference to economics already covered by the Common Market. The greatest opposition to the French plan came from the Dutch, who, however, were prepared to accept it provided Britain were included. The discussions of the Fouchet Committee broke down in 1962 and have not been resumed. Since then various governments have put forward plans for breaking the deadlock, and at the end of 1964 the Dutch withdrew their insistence on Britain's inclusion. But the French have refused to show any interest in political union, other than as a lever to put pressure on her partners in connection with the common agricultural policy. And as far as defence is concerned the divisions between the Six or rather between France and her five partners are of course even greater.

It is clear then that no real progress in the defence and foreign political fields is likely for some time – at least until General de Gaulle goes. All through the talks on political union the EEC Commission has shown very little interest in them. And it is undoubtedly right in its view that a European union will succeed or fail by the integration of the economies of the member countries, and compared with which the success or failure of the various plans for a rather rudimentary form of political union is of lesser importance. This does not mean that with goodwill some reinvigoration of Western European Union might not be effected which would itself provide the basis of a political community. But it does mean that the central problem is still the successful development of the EEC and the relationship to it of the states of the EFTA, and in the first instance, of Britain. Here we come up against the apparent policy and presumptive intentions of the present ruler of France.

CHAPTER SIX

*

De Gaulle and the 'Europe des Etats'

THE President of France has publicly proclaimed his mortality. Unlikely and unwelcome though the possibility may be, and is, this chapter may therefore be out of date by the time the book appears. *'La garde quiveille aux barrières du Louvre n'en défend point nos Roi.'* It may not, however, be altogether irrelevant, even in the distressing event of the disappearance of the General from the political scene. For his views on the European Idea (which in its supra-national form he vigorously opposes) are shared by many people, not only in France, but also, chiefly among the older generation, in Britain and elsewhere. They are consequently of abiding interest. For they may even be applied by lesser men in France after the great man's departure.

In considering the problem, therefore, the first thing to remember that, as we all know and as he himself believes, de Gaulle *is* France. When he studies the dossier of the European Economic Community he naturally draws on his ancestral memory. What does this tell him? Chapter One has given us a clue. That Europe, that 'Christendom' rather, should in some way be united under the leadership of France, the geographical centre, the intellectual hub, the real heir, whatever the pretensions of the German tribes, to the figurative mantle of the Empire. France, and France alone as the poet said is 'the mother of arts, of arms and of laws'. This is what Charlemagne tells him, even though he did live at Aachen; this is no doubt the advice of Saint Louis also; this, the General is certainly informed, is the conviction of the Grand Monarque;

69

this is the real secret of the tremendous Corsican. What do the other great defenders of France think about the Common Market – Richelieu himself or Turenne or the Constable of Bourbon? It is easy to imagine: God himself, they used to say, acts through the Franks – '*Gesta Dei per Francos*'.

In a very real sense, therefore, as the General sees it, France *is* Europe. If France is stricken, so is Christendom. Without France Christendom cannot exist. France, or rather Paris, is the centre: the rest is the periphery. What is Germany? Still only partially civilized and 'Christian': thus a danger, if unified; preferably a collection of states rather than a state; happiest when the Western part turns confidently towards its sun. What is Italy? A country with many virtues, but never a nation. Spain? For three hundred years she has simply lived on her great memories. L'Angleterre? Ah, that is a difficulty. Britain is a great nation. It cannot be denied that she is also European. But only partially. Did not Churchill himself tell him that, if forced to choose, Britain would prefer the Ocean to Europe? It follows that this island must give her first loyalty to her Commonwealth and indeed be drawn, if only because of the common language, more closely towards the daughter, America, who after all is now grown up and must live her own life. Perhaps one day Britain will begin to turn in earnest towards the real fount of civilization. But not now. Surely not now. As for poor hungry Russia, well she is not really a menace and can therefore safely be used as a counterweight to overcome the irritating reluctance of the Germans to break with America and accept French political and nuclear supremacy. When, however, they do, Europe can once again resume her essential world 'civilizing mission', and the centre of Europe is naturally France.

It will be seen that under this conception Paris is not only the centre of Europe, it is also the centre of the world. There are even many citations from the General's speeches which could be used as evidence for his belief that it is the centre of the Universe. What is certain is that there can be no question of France becoming something other than France. Hence the General's constant pre-occupation with the possible loss of national identity. For if France is in any way, or to any degree merged in a greater whole, even in a greater European whole, the kernel of the nut is as it were softened and the whole fruit is therefore likely to rot. Thus gallo-centrism, or gaullo-centrism (for since de Gaulle *is* France, the two expressions are identical) is not, as some might think, an endearing quirk in the make-up of a great personality: it is part and parcel of the man. But it is more than that. It is that very philosophy of a nationalism which cannot accept what, in our modern jargon, we call 'an element of supra-nationality'. If Europe is to come closer together, and the General is no doubt perfectly sincere in wishing that it should, it can only be on the basis of a co-operation between nation-states, of which France will be the most ancient, the most distinguished, and if possible, the most powerful. It is true that France may 'die' as an entity. As he himself told me during his period in the wilderness she very nearly did so during the last war: but if France does 'die' then there is no hope for Europe. A vague collection of international bureaucrats – a *'méli-mélo'* in his own memorable phrase – will attempt to govern the ancient nations of Europe and such an attempt is bound to fail. Since there can be no common patriotism there will be no directing force or will. After a confused period of parliamentary wrangling among the politicians of the old type an impossible situation will arise. As in the Paulskirche in 1848, force of some kind would no doubt be applied by somebody. If France fell out, perhaps it might even be applied one day (dreadful thought) by Germany. All these considerations seem, on the face of it, to be present in the General's mind. Great man as he is, he does not conceal his fundamental convictions and objectives. Only his tactics necessarily remain obscure. The end, by his own confession, is constant.

These convictions are not negligible: they must be taken very seriously. For they are views firmly rooted in the unstated assumptions not only of France, but *mutatis mutandis*, of those of other great nations. It is the nation-state talking. And from the end of the sixteenth century until 1958 no limitation on the nation-state's absolute authority in Europe was ever voluntarily accepted. If as Aristotle said 'infinite time is the maker of states,' it is arguable that about twenty years is too short a period for the construction of a super-state. All this will not necessarily convince, but it may suffice to show that it is not so much the exaggerations, the idiosyncrasies of the General's approach that matter, it is the appeal to ancient and powerful instincts which exist in all our European lands and are by no means dead yet. De Gaulle could not be still where he is if his nationalist foreign policy did not have strong support in France. An inspired leader with an 'anglocentric' philosophy might well have similar support in Britain, or his counter-part (*absit omen!*) in the Fatherland.

For it must be admitted that the Leader well knows the mentality of his own country. Indeed, since he is himself France, this is in no way surprising. One very marked feature of this great nation is what is called *la méfiance*, that is to say a fundamental mistrust and a refusal to take anything for granted. An aspect of this is a tendency to search for hidden motives in any proposal made, more particularly proposals coming from foreigners. There is a story of the French representative at an international conference after the Napoleonic Wars who was particularly suspicious of his Russian colleague. Bag after bag contained accounts of the dubious manoeuvres and dark designs of this able diplomatist. Finally a despatch arrived at the Quai d'Orsy which began as follows: 'The Russian Ambassador died today. I ask myself what was his motive?'

Coupled with such suspicion is a tremendous realistic toughness. The motto of Frenchmen is '*il faut se défendre*', you must look out for yourself or other people will do you in. All this is a source of great inner strength, though it does often result in the French being difficult partners. But it also means that if the French can be harnessed to an idea (and it must be their own idea) they will do their magnificent best to support it. In their present Gaullist mood they may not accept the European Idea. But if Britain were really committed to it that would affect them profoundly — provided it was a genuine conversion and not just another trick of 'perfidious Albion'.

Looked at from a not very different angle de Gaulle is in many ways the embodiment of Macchiavelli's 'Prince'. The object of the Prince was to keep himself in power and he was, in his relations with other Princes, not influenced in any way by the 'ought to be' but only by the 'is'. De Gaulle's early work *Le Fil de l'Epée* is evidence that he had absorbed many of the essential precepts of Macchiavelli. Thus he is secret and devious; he is ruthless; and he knows at the same time when to placate a difficult opposition by playing it off against another school of thought. Perhaps the original Prince might have thought the General's mystical ideas about the rôle of his own nation-state a little unrealistic if not dangerous: but basically the lessons have been very well applied.

In any case, if it is generally acceptable, my description of de Gaulle's attitude solves many riddles. Whether something or other is in the apparent interest of France from a material point of view is an entirely secondary consideration. The criterion by which it is judged is whether it increases France's status in the world – her *'rang'* – and hence, by extension, the status of the General, who is the embodiment of France herself. In the light of his 'historic nationalism' the famous passage in his Memoirs in which he contemplated forming a Third Force in Western Europe and associating this now with America and now with Russia, which seemed so fantastic at the time is at least explicable. So is his intense dislike of NATO, not because (as some think) he did not devise it himself, but simply because France does not occupy therein a central or commanding position. Under this interpretation of his attitude all his gestures fit into place: the original attempt in 1960 to enter the 'Western Great Power Club', even though France had not then exploded a nuclear device; the subsequent effort, after toying with the idea of a Franco-German-British combination, to become the sole valid ally of a divided (and therefore satellite) Germany; the spectacular French nuclear policy; the veto; the generous aid programme; the plan to dethrone the dollar and the pound as the sole international currencies; the courting of Latin America; the flirtation with the Soviet Union; the recognition of

73

China; the demand for a neutralization of all Vietnam; the call for some new 'balance' in the world. All these gestures, sensible though some of them may have been, were primarily designed to make an impression and to put France on the map. Most could be effected without infuriating the allies too much. The French themselves got nothing very tangible out of them – only a certain pleasure in seeing the allies disconcerted; but in a mystical way the stock of France certainly went up. The real triumph of the General in the foreign field was the 'liberation' of Algeria and the old French Empire. And this, admirable though it was, came about in a way entirely contrary to his original declared intention.

Indeed in a more general way the thing to remember about de Gaulle's policies is that though the aim, namely, the greater glory of France, remains constant there is no consistent long-term policy for attaining that end. There is, to be just, one refrain that has been heard for a long time in the General's speeches even though it has only lately been promoted to the status of a major political objective fitting in with the pro-Russian mood of the hour. It is really part of the 'Third Force' plan previously mentioned. This is the conception of 'Europe from the Atlantic to the Urals'. So far as one can make out, this slogan embodies the idea that Christendom is, not only geographically, but also historically and as it were spiritually, more akin to Russia than America. It therefore fits in very well with the spontaneous anti-American sentiment in France which has such obvious present political advantage. But if it is to be taken seriously it must perforce imply that some kind of European association will eventually be constructed which will include the Russians. We have already seen in an earlier chapter what a strange notion this would be if it ever were put into effect. But again, if the phrase is to be taken literally, it can only mean that, while Russia is to be included, Britain is to be kept out. (At the very least, the General has never said, when elaborating on the plan, that he wants Britain to be inside rather than outside.) Thus the idea would presumably be to try to organize Europe on the basis of some Franco-Soviet deal providing for the reunification of Germany after the departure of the Americans, on lines agreeable to both parties. If this is not so then the real object should be stated. I myself queried the whole conception in a speech at Lyons on 8 March 1965, and my theme was not, I think, repudiated in any serious French non-Gaullist organ. If indeed it means anything – which is perhaps doubtful – the phrase is highly sinister.

But how even in theory do the non-French, whether allies or not, fit into a Gaullocentric system? This has never been clear. What would happen if other members of the Western Alliance – including the Germans – applied to themselves the same sort of historical criteria as the General applies to his own nation? Nobody knows. The only possible (Gaullist) answer is that they would not be entitled to do so because, objectively considered, France, by reason of her history, is different from and indeed superior to her friends and neighbours. The non-French ought to recognize that France from the time of Clovis has been singled out, perhaps divinely, for a very special civilizing mission.

Can, therefore, this special people contemplate entering into any European association which depends for its successful operation on some limited form of majority voting and on paying some respect in certain distinct spheres to the decisions of a democratically elected parliament? The extraordinary thing is that anyone should have imagined that the General would ever admit that it could. For so long as Gaullist principles are maintained France cannot and will not carry out the plain letter of the Treaty of Rome. Probably therefore when the legal necessity of accepting the system of majority voting arises the General will seize on some excuse for holding it up, or at least continue on the assumption that the system could never apply to France which could not endure the humiliation of ever being placed by a minority. The idea apparently is that the Community can somehow, as it were, be put into cold storage and not allowed to develop beyond a certain point. But if this does not work, then the General will have no hesitation in drawing the legitimate consequences. France's allies will have failed to see the light, France will therefore rightly re-assume her entire freedom of action. We shall all start again from scratch and then *'par la force même des choses'* a new European system will arise in which the other Europeans will agree that France, having now recovered her ancient *grandeur* is the natural and undisputed leader of the Continent.*

There is no need to be astonished at such a conclusion. For it is one which must be reached by any one of the larger European states if it really adopts a nationalistic policy. An equally good case could be made out for British or German leadership of Western Europe. It probably only needs a statesman or a demagogue of genius to persuade either nation that this is so. In no case, if Gaullist principles are themselves applied could either Germany or Britain accept French leadership. Consequently we arrive at the point at which the previous chapter ended. The British principle, stoutly maintained between 1945 and 1961 that all co-operation is desirable short of any kind of supra-nationality, would have to be reverted to, and all efforts to unify the Continent by consent would have to be abandoned. Whether it would eventually be unified by force applied from within or without would be left to the future to determine. More likely it would be unified by pressure from without. More likely still it could remain permanently divided and thus under the influence of the one super-power and the other.

This can hardly be the conclusion reached by General de Gaulle. He must presumably believe that he has a real chance of establishing what he calls a *Europe des Etats* (preferably without Britain at any rate for many years), in other words of establishing what would actually be a sort of 'Greater France'. It is quite true that this structure, if it could be achieved, and more especially if it were joined by Austria and Denmark and were in association with Spain would be an imposing one of some 235 million people, greater therefore than either the USA or the Soviet Union. But in order to exert its strength whether economically or politically, in the foreign field it would have to speak with one voice: and if there were no machinery for arriving at collective decisions other than complete unanimity, this

* Written before the dramatic events of 30 June 1965.

76

voice could only be that of the leader, France. No doubt the able French diplomats and specialists would often be able to arrive at some sort of consensus. The final decisions would, however, always be taken in Paris. More particularly this would be true in the nuclear field and indeed in foreign policy generally. There is no other conceivable way in which such a system could work. The paradox is that whereas de Gaulle indignantly rejects an Atlantic system in which one state, America, has a leading rôle by virtue of her possession of great nuclear and indeed economic superiority, he proposes for Europe, a similar system in which one nation, namely, France, has a leading rôle, and this in spite of the fact that she is less important both economically and numerically than either Western Germany or Britain, or indeed (if numbers only should count) even Italy, and only possesses an embryonic nuclear force, deprived of any early warning apparatus, which by itself is quite unlikely to terrify either the USA or the Soviet Union. Even in ten years' time, when and if it is largely under-water it is hard to believe that it will be of any great importance as a deterrent.

In conversation with de Gaulle whom I saw after a long interval in September 1964 and again at the funeral of Sir Winston Churchill, I have over the years always done my best to suggest that a Western Europe without Britain does not make any political sense; that an attempt to form it would probably only lead in the long run, not to French but to German or alternatively to Russian domination of Western Europe; that however that may be, no political system acceptable to any of France's neighbours can possibly work unless there is some machinery for common decision-taking other than unanimity; that by far the best thing would be for the French and the British to agree on the formation of a European political and defence machine which would embody this principle, if only, to start off with, in a very restricted way; and that one of the first tasks of such a nucleus should be to prepare a scheme for the co-ordination of our two *Forces de Frappe* and of all the conventional forces of Western Europe within the framework of the Western Alliance. I do not think de Gaulle is entirely unsympathetic to this kind of reasoning but he is inhibited by his apparently quite genuine fear of losing his 'national identity'. We therefore invariably come up against the rock of 'sovereignty'. He will accept nothing, so he always says, which has the faintest 'element of supra-nationality'. And of course on the other hand if Britain should come into a simple *Europe des Etats*, which she might be willing to do as such, would it not be inevitable that the leadership would fall from France's grasp? The ancestral voices win.

Though, as I say, I have the impression that the General would really prefer to come to terms with l'Angleterre I really do not see how we can escape from this basic dilemma. It is true that if, as many allege, he is intent, if not on actually wrecking the EEC, at any rate on putting it into cold storage, we ought to be able to fix up some new kind of European Community out of the débris; but we cannot do this on the basis of a *Europe des Etats*, and as long as this concept is insisted upon there will simply be increasing European anarchy from which only the Soviet Union, or China, can possibly profit. French withdrawal from the EEC and indeed from NATO is not something which even the most anti-Gaullist European could possibly desire for it would lead to a division in the alliance. No wonder the Kremlin is increasingly delighted by the General's policies.

There are people in Britain who are prepared to justify them too. This cannot be attributable solely to a pleasure in being kicked around, though no doubt that comes into it. The approval is probably due to a genuine conviction that a United Europe in a supra-national sense is an illusion and that the sooner we ourselves pursue a purely nationalist policy the better. So far as we are concerned we should, therefore, as the General would wish, leave the organization of Europe to him, and apart from special joint projects, get on with developing our Commonwealth and Empire. I think de Gaulle has always been genuinely astonished that the successors to Sir Winston Churchill have not taken this simple course. Indeed he once told me himself that he could not believe that we would ever sacrifice 'our wonderful system of Imperial Preferences'. Unfortunately, as we shall see later, this is not a practicable solution. The Empire has ceased to exist. The Commonwealth, though of great value as a sort of interracial club, is not, and cannot be, either a political or an economic entity. The proportion of our trade with the Commonwealth decreases yearly, more and more countries like Australia and New Zealand will be obliged to trade with the great industrial complex of Japan. To a lesser extent, but the argument holds so far as it goes, it is as if we suggested to de Gaulle that he should get on with the development of his own 'commonwealth', more trade with Indo-China and the vast 'French' districts of Africa, closer relations with Algeria, Tunisia and Morocco, and so on. No doubt he would like to; but just as in our case there are nationalist considerations which prevent any such development. Of course we can, and we should, by means which I may dwell on later, bring the Commonwealth together as much as we can and in particular try to bring it into some kind of special relationship with a United Europe: but to suggest that it can be a substitute for the latter is not to compare like with like. If Europe remains divided the Commonwealth does not provide, for us, any satisfactory alternative.

Now, if de Gaulle, owing to his evident inability to accept the underlying thesis of the EEC, is really going to wreck the development of the European Common Market all this would hardly apply. A new situation would arise and we should all have to do the best we could in the circumstances. But it is unlikely that the General would go as far as this, even if he could, or that he would want to. The great industrial complex will probably thus continue to gain ground, though less rapidly than it otherwise would, our own exclusion from it having an increasingly unfortunate effect, not only for us but for Europe generally. And if it does continue, then whatever de Gaulle may do or say, it will one day produce some kind of political authority.

It is in fact quite possible that we are all taking the recent attitudes of de Gaulle too tragically. The apparent nihilism is no doubt principally designed to delight the more unsuspecting of the French and thus to persuade them to keep the General in office. There is, as I have already suggested, no such thing as 'Gaullism' as a philosophy, still less as a policy. The Gaullists simply say hurray to whatever the General from time to time tells them to do or think. To have boxed the compass several times in foreign policy within seven years is no mean feat. In so doing to have been treated as an 'infallible guide' by a large majority of the sceptical Gauls is even more astonishing. The only guiding line through all this is, I repeat, to grasp that whatever France does is right; that the General *is* France; that therefore the General is infallible. Apparent contradictions or anomalies in French foreign policy cannot therefore be taken at their face value. They are *tours de force*, designed to astonish the bourgeois, performed in perfect safety to a dazzled audience over the useful safety net of American nuclear supremacy.

Whatever the difficulties therefore in the way of achieving a United Europe, or at any rate a United Western Europe may be, that is to say some Europe other than a *Europe des Etats* which, as we have seen, even if it were achievable, would not really be a Europe at all, but only a Greater France, it looks as if they would be generally overcome. It may be a slower process than we imagine. It is true that we shall have, before any meaningful political authority is established, to create, if not exactly a European patriotism, at least a European fellow feeling and a European sense of purpose. Among the 'establishments' and the intellectuals, this may be a reasonably easy process. Perhaps in those circles the Homo Europaeus, so suspect to the General, may be said to have already arrived. For the people as a whole this evolution will clearly be a great deal slower. But the broad impression, among those qualified to gather the evidence, is that the tendency in all the European lands, the groundswell as it were, is towards some real unity and against the nationalist, the atavistic instincts that push them in a contrary direction. Towering genius though he is, it does not look, on present form, as if de Gaulle would be able to hold back for long the forces making for unity. Certainly his successor, however nationalistically minded, would have far greater difficulty than he in repeating King Canute's well-known gesture. So it may well, at this point, be advisable for us to see why it is that thinking in Gaullist terms, tempting though it may be for an ex-Imperial power such as Britain, is no longer adapted to the problems of our time, and what the real reasons are which still push us, however reluctantly, towards acceptance of membership of a genuine and vital European Community.

CHAPTER SEVEN

*

The Reasons Why

LET us therefore now set out once again as shortly and as clearly as possible, the immediate reasons, both economic and political, which still suggest that Britain should be well advised to join the European Economic Community as soon as she can, together with the contrary arguments. (There is no reason to examine the special positions of the other candidates – Denmark, Norway and Ireland – who would almost certainly join too if we successfully prepared the way.) Let us first take the economic reasons.

ECONOMIC ADVANTAGES

(*a*) From the point of view of the United Kingdom the main economic argument for our actually joining the EEC is that by so doing we should enlarge our home market for the sale of our industrial products. (The Commonwealth for the most part puts duties on these products, and even our preferences are fast disappearing.) At present therefore our 'home market' consists in principle of the British Isles plus the other members of the EFTA, though complete free trade within this area has not as yet been established, and the whole system was imperilled recently by the application of a fifteen per cent surcharge on EFTA goods imported into the United Kingdom. This 'home market' however, only amounts to about ninety-five million people in all – i.e. about fifty-four million in the United Kingdom and another forty million or so in the other countries of EFTA

82

– and it is true that imports from the other members into Portugal will be subjected to considerable restrictions for some time to come. It is further true that Austria (population about eight million) is at the time of writing in negotiation with the EEC, and it is possible that she may actually leave EFTA for the other camp in the reasonably near future. Nor can the attitude of Denmark by any means be taken for granted. There is strong support in Denmark for membership with the EEC rather than with EFTA. A loose association of rather disparate countries which may not number in practice much more than eighty million could hardly therefore compare with the largely integrated economies of the Six, at the moment comprising something like 180 million people and possibly 200 million fairly soon.

The industrialized countries of the world will thus, if things go on as at present, be divided into four main groups, namely, the Soviet Union and the countries of the Comecon amounting in all to well over 300 million people; the United States, with which to a large extent are associated Canada and even to some extent Japan, that is to say 190 million in close association with another 120 million, in other words 310 million in all; the countries of the EEC, namely, 180–200 million in association with Greece and Turkey, that is anything up to 230 million in all; and the United Kingdom with a 'home market' (including EFTA) which might vary between 80 and 95 million only. It must again be emphasized that the Commonwealth unfortunately cannot now count in any way as a 'home market' owing to the rapid demobilization of the old system of 'Imperial Preferencies' and for the tendency of individual members of the Commonwealth to trade more and more with countries other than the United Kingdom. What remains of the old system is useful and would serve to cushion the shock occasioned by our increasing isolation, but within a few years it will be seen that we shall have few greater advantages in Commonwealth countries than most other industrialized states.

In these circumstances it must be obvious that British industry will be increasingly at a disadvantage when it comes to streamlining and rationalizing itself in order to be able to compete in world markets with greater and increasingly efficient industries such as for example the American motor industry, computers, aeroplanes, chemical products, and so on. Only by assuring itself of a larger home market (or alternatively by actually producing within another home market which has certain obvious long-term disadvantages) can British industry maintain its competitive power and produce the goods which can be sold abroad in order to pay for the imports and raw materials and foodstuffs on which the population of these islands depends. Only so in practice can inefficient and unprofitable concerns be weeded out and restrictive practices of all kinds in all sections of industry be removed through the necessity of competing in some vast new industrial area. That something is holding back British industry is made clear by the simple fact that between 1956 (that is *after* German recovery) and 1964 the proportion of world trade held by Britain dropped from 9·4 per cent to 8·1 per cent while that of Germany increased from 8·9 per cent to 10·7 per cent.

It is sometimes asked, why, if it is primarily a question of joining a larger whole, not join some Atlantic Common Market – in other words go into a customs union with America, as recently recommended by Senator Javits? This might indeed one day be a solution, but at the moment it is just not on. There is little reason to suppose that Congress would now welcome the great competition of British exports in certain fields any more than we should welcome the competition of US exports in others. If joining the EEC would mean an upheaval in the United Kingdom, joining America in present conditions would involve a far greater upheaval. We might gradually get nearer the USA in many ways if we cannot get into Europe but the process would have to be a gradual one. If we do get into Europe the whole process of getting closer to America will be facilitated (see Chapter 9).

(*b*) In addition to the obviously unhealthy long-term effect on British industry if it is confined to a relatively small industrial area is the obvious fact that short of almost impossible progress in the direction of abolition of tariffs on a world-wide scale British goods will be at an increasing disadvantage in one of their most rapidly expanding markets, namely that of the present Community of the Six. The percentage of British trade with the Six has in fact risen from 13·8 per cent to 18·2 per cent during the period 1958 to 1964; the percentage of British trade with the Commonwealth during the same period has fallen from 38·6 per cent to 29·8 per cent.

(*c*) There is no doubt in any case that for such time as we remain outside the rapidly forming industrial bloc in Western Europe the long-term position of sterling will not be strong and we shall be incapable of accumulating those reserves without which we shall neither be able to maintain our military presence in Germany or our presence anywhere else in the world, to say nothing of contributing as we should to direct aid to the various underdeveloped countries.

(*d*) Then again, whatever the National Farmers' Union may collectively say, and whatever the disadvantages may be from the point of view of some producers and British economy generally, there is no doubt that certain sections of British agriculture would benefit very greatly by entry into the European Common Market. There is no reason to suppose that efficient farmers would do anything but benefit by selling their cereals at something like £38 a ton (though of course we should hope that this price might be sensibly diminished in the course of time). And there is no need to suppose that efficient farmers in Britain should not also be able to produce bacon, butter, eggs, cheese and milk at the prices which now seem about to be negotiated within the countries of the Six, provided always of course that effectively the same price is charged throughout the enlarged union for imported grain and feeding stuffs, as it would be.

(*e*) Finally, it can well be argued that unless some kind of economic community emerges in Western Europe as a whole and is able to speak with one voice it will be more difficult for the International Monetary Fund, under the scheme proposed by Professor Triffin, or indeed under any other scheme, to secure the necessary majority which will be necessary if such an authority is to take crucial decisions in the realm of international liquidity.

ECONOMIC DISADVANTAGES

As against these advantages the following arguments can certainly be adduced:

(*a*) As regards agriculture, if we came into the EEC we should have to levy duties on imports of foodstuffs coming from abroad – including imports from Commonwealth countries – although we should hope to arrange for some transitional period for some of these. This would mean that the difference between the world price of (say) wheat at £26 a ton and the Common Market price at present fixed at £38 a ton would have to be paid by the importer to the common farming fund. Since we import something like half our foodstuffs, the levies in the United Kingdom would be greater even than those levied in Germany, which also imports a large proportion of her foodstuffs. But one of the major difficulties would be that whereas we should indeed save most of the £350 million odd which is now produced out of the budget by the tax payer for the purpose of 'deficiency payments' and other subsidies to our farmers so that they may compete with imported foodstuffs sold at the world price here, we should under the new arrangement, not be able to keep the proceeds of the levies but would have to transfer them to the Commission in Brussels where they would be divided up in accordance with some agreed plan for the encouragement of European agriculture generally. Unless no relief is given therefore, it seems likely, on the face of it, that we should be called upon to do considerable damage to our trade with the Commonwealth and at the same time to subsidize to some extent continental agriculture at the expense of our own. This would not matter tremendously as such, since, the hard wheat of Canada (for instance) which is not produced in Europe would be likely to be imported in any case, whereas we might hope that some special arrangements, if only of a temporary character, might be applied to Australian soft wheat and to dairy produce from New Zealand. Everyone admits that this point must be the subject of a major negotiation, just as it is at present the subject of a negotiation within the Community itself where the amount of the levies which Germany or Italy will retain and not hand over to the Community has not been settled at the moment of writing. Moreover, in a general way, if European agricultural production is artificially stimulated beyond a certain point trade between the Community as a whole and the outside world is bound to be unfavourably affected. The European price of grain is obviously therefore a matter of major importance which should if possible be the subject of negotiation before our entry.

(b) There is also the disputed question of the prospective increase in the cost of living in the United Kingdom supposing that some such system were ever applied. This argument has probably been exaggerated by those who do not wish us to come into the EEC in any circumstances. Nobody seems to think that it would be more than about seven per cent and some economists maintain that it would be considerably less than that owing to the possibility of an increase in food prices being compensated by a decrease (owing to the large market) in the prices of certain industrial products. We should also of course be able, if we so desired, to cut taxes as a result of saving on the deficiency payments or subsidize the underprivileged. Still if there were a considerable increase it would no doubt force wages up *pro tanto* and thus slightly diminish our competitive power in world markets. This argument must be balanced against the general damage to our balance of payments if we cannot join the Market and our competitive power is for that reason seriously diminished. It must also be recognized that even as we are wages seem to be going up by about seven per cent per annum, anyhow, though how this can be reconciled with a planned three per cent annual increase in the Gross National Product is what foreigners call an 'English mystery'.

(*c*) It is also arguable that, unless special arrangements were arrived at, immediate entry into the Common Market by the United Kingdom would give rise to almost intolerable stresses and strains. Some smaller industries might find themselves in a bad situation; there might even be a balance of payments crisis; there could be some temporary unemployment. But as against this (and apart from the fact that the disappearance of some highly uneconomic firms might well be a very good thing) it could be said that Britain's entry if it ever came about would no doubt be undertaken gradually and that in any case a balance of payments crisis would really be impossible in the circumstances since none of the other members could afford to see the currency, even of a prospective member, being seriously affected.

(*d*) Finally, it is rightly alleged that if we came into the Common Market without the agreement of our EFTA partners we might, apart from straining our contractual obligations, run the risk of losing on the swings something of what we had gained on the roundabouts. If we do come in it should therefore be in agreement with our EFTA partners some of whom would come in with us, others being no doubt able to arrange suitable Articles of Association. But it should be noted that the EFTA Treaty does contain a twelve-month denunciation clause.

On balance, the economic disadvantages appear to be pretty heavily outweighed by the advantages provided – and it is of course a big proviso – that there is a measure of understanding and indeed co-operation on the part of the members of the present EEC.

We should here for a moment no doubt also discuss the argument that the EEC if enlarged would be nothing but a 'rich white man's club' principally designed to keep the terms of trade weighted against the underdeveloped countries, and thus to perpetuate the worst form of neo-colonialism resulting in the rich getting richer and the poor getting poorer. There is no doubt that any system whereby such aid as is given to the under-developed countries is counter-balanced or even more than counter-balanced by a drop in the world price of, for example, coffee or tin is indefensible, and that it is up to the richer nations in some way to take action against this trend, either by directly relating aid to the terms of trade, or by some kind of long-term world commodity agreements. What is not evident is why the formation of a larger trading area in Western Europe and the beginning of some political authority in that area should encourage this lamentable trend. On the contrary it must be supposed that, more especially if Britain joined the EEC, the whole policy in this respect would be centrally devised and enormous benefits resulting from a larger market should result in a sensible and generous policy of aid. Indeed one of the chief points of such a European Union would be to harmonize the policies of all the ex-Imperial powers in the interests of a progressive and liberal relationship between them and the so-called emergent countries.

POLITICAL ADVANTAGES

(*a*) If the Western Alliance is to continue it must either take the form of an association between one elephant – the United States – and a number of very much smaller animals inevitably led in all important respects by the elephant itself (with consequent psychological difficulties), or some kind of partnership depending for its successful operation on the creation of two 'pillars' – one in the East and one in the West. The reason for this is that if there are three pillars, that is so say America, Europe and the United Kingdom in association with a few Commonwealth and other countries, the latter will not be of the same magnitude as the other two and consequently the 'tripod' will be unstable. Moreover, quite apart from that it will be impossible to form a Western European pillar without the United Kingdom because neither France nor Germany is prepared to admit that one of them should be in the lead, and at the same time neither is at present prepared to contemplate a really effective political union involving a pooled leadership. Only therefore if the United Kingdom is associated directly – and preferably in some form of union – with France and Germany, can there be any question of a European partner in the Atlantic Alliance. Thus it is only by first solving the European equation that we can establish the continuing validity of the Western Alliance on any basis other than an acknowledged and accepted American hegemony.

(*b*) If for one reason or another Britain cannot join the European Economic Community and form some kind of political and defence community together with it, it seems quite possible that the alliance will be chiefly based on some kind of German/American understanding, in which Britain will by the nature of things be a rather junior partner. Assuming that in these circumstances the Franco-German Treaty is of no value and that France even retires from the Western Alliance a situation will be created in Western Europe from which obviously only the Soviet Union could benefit. We cannot, it is true, absolutely ensure that the situation does not arise, but if we could at least indicate our desire to join a Western European political and defence organization with full powers within the Alliance, we might be able to prevent the adoption of very dangerous policies across the Channel.

(*c*) In any case, only by the formation of some autonomous Western Europe (always within the Alliance) which one day might perhaps be sufficiently strong to defend itself, can any German reunification ever take place 'in peace and freedom'. For such reunification clearly is only conceivable in the event of the withdrawal both of American and of Russian troops to their own countries, and such a withdrawal could only take place when neither the Soviet Union nor America has any reason to fear that Europe, which would of course include some reunification of the German peoples, would either be a menace in itself or likely to come wholly under the domination of one super-power or the other.

(*d*) It may well be long before such a situation can arise and in the meantime, even if France defects, the Western Alliance is likely to continue. If Europe is ever fully formed involving a reunified Germany and the establishment of free régimes in the countries of Eastern Europe it is rather difficult to see what exactly the Alliance's rôle would be. But it is obvious that a 'wider Europe' of this kind will take many years to achieve, even if it is ever possible to do so. If it were to be formed it is by no means certain where the centre of power would be and how it would be organized. All such possibilities, however, are dependent on the previous coming-together in some real sense of at least some European nations and, as things are, this could only happen in the West to start off with. The formation of the Western European nucleus, in other words, is something on which everything else depends.

POLITICAL DISADVANTAGES

(*a*) It is sometimes suggested that if Britain and the other applicants came into the EEC and thereafter established a Political and Defence Community Britain would be 'freezing the status quo' and making any larger European union impossible. In particular, according to this school of thought, the danger would be the creation of another independent super-state in the west of Europe which, by the nature of things, would have to pursue a totally independent policy and hence assume its own defence, a task of which it would not be capable. Therefore you might not only have a disruption of the present Western Alliance, but also make it impossible either to reunify Germany or to come to some sensible arrangement with the other states of Europe. A variant of this argument is that the accession of Britain might prejudice the possibility of creating a 'nuclear free zone' in Central Europe as a first step towards possible general disarmament.

(*b*) According to others, we should even be well advised to abandon all attempts to come into the EEC ourselves and actually help France together with a more or less satellite Germany to negotiate some German settlement directly with the Soviet Union. Withdrawal of British and American troops from Germany would be one of the pre-conditions of such a policy.

All these reasons for keeping out of any Western European union are of dubious validity. As we have seen under the political advantages, the best way for arranging the ultimate reunification of the Germans would be the formation of some Western European entity which, in the long run, would be capable of an independent existence, though it is sincerely to be hoped that it would continue to be a corporate member of the Western Alliance. The grave defect of the second line of argument is obviously that France and Germany, if they were acting for an integrated EEC – wholly improbable for the time being – would simply not be strong enough to negotiate with the Soviet Union if deprived of American and indeed of British support. There is really no reason why the West should play the Russian game even though we may ultimately hope that, perhaps under pressure created by the breach with China, the Soviet Union may become increasingly well disposed and allow the satellite or ex-satellite states in Eastern Europe an increasing measure of political and economic freedom.

As for the nuclear free zone in Central Europe, that is really a function of disarmament and can hardly be dissociated from that problem. If adopted it would presumably mean that the rôle of 'tactical' nuclear weapons in a war originating on the line of division in Germany would be lessened and that of the 'strategic' weapons increased. That is, if the American Army continues to be stationed in Germany. For then it would seem that the absence of nuclear weapons in its area might increase the danger of rapid escalation, and that, in effect, the French doctrine of an immediate and total nuclear response to any aggression would prevail. However this may be, it is difficult to see how the possibility of creating a nuclear free zone can be used as an argument against Britain going into Europe. If we ever did join the EEC, the chances of our ever establishing such a zone could not appear to be prejudiced one way or the other.

Even if we conclude that, apart from historical and social

reasons, the balance of advantage seems still to lie pretty heavily in the direction of our actually joining the EEC, we must admit that for some time which might be measured in months, more likely in years, we shall not, owing to French opposition, be able to achieve our objective. It has therefore been suggested that we should do well to 'build bridges' between the EEC and EFTA in the hope that eventually we shall be able in some way to amalgamate the two systems. Nobody in their senses would object to any measures which have the effect of tempering the difficulties produced by the division of Western Europe into two economic blocs, provided we realize that all such measures would simply be palliatives pending the emergence of governments in France and Britain which with the other member states would jointly be responsible for extending the Community to include this country and the other applicants. It can also quite legitimately be said that, if we do want to come into the Common Market it is perhaps unwise to go too far in the direction of giving the French advantages which they would otherwise only expect to get if we did so.

We must also admit that the proposed 'bridges' lend themselves rather to practical measures of co-operation and less ambitious schemes for negotiations between the two institutions. In the first category come such schemes as the Channel Tunnel (or rather a bridge, if you really want to build bridges), co-operation between British and French – and it is to be hoped also with German and Italian – aircraft industries; the gradual adoption by this country of the metric system; co-operation in nuclear matters other than military; possible agreement on the reduction of certain tariffs within the framework of GATT and practical schemes of this order. In the second category come suggestions for actual negotiations, if only of a minor character between Common Market officials and those of EFTA. This would be difficult and even dangerous since EFTA is not and can hardly be a customs union, still less an economic union, and therefore cannot pursue a common policy or indulge, as an entity, in any high level negotiations. Moreover, it is certain that the French at any rate will be suspicious of such a manoeuvre, thinking that here again was a plot to merge the Community of the Six in some larger whole, thereby reducing it to something like a free trade area. Nor is it only the French who might have such suspicions but most of the members of the Economic Commission in Brussels as well as 'Europeans' generally.

It might well be different if the British and other EFTA governments said that it was their definite intention to sign the Treaty as soon as possible, as soon that is as there is any evidence of goodwill on the other side of the Channel. Pending the renewal of negotiations which would of course in the long run be necessary, there might well be adjustments which could suitably be made in the economy of the EFTA nations concerned, including Britain and perhaps corresponding adjustments in all or some of the members of the Six. Whether even then negotiations between EFTA as a body and the EEC would be possible is, however, open to grave doubt. Almost undoubtedly the best method would be for the British to make the necessary explorations in the first instance, and then having got to a certain stage, arrange for the entry of other applicants, Articles of Association for Sweden, Switzerland and Portugal to be considered in the light of progress made. In this way the main objective as described above could always be kept before our eyes and the reasons of general European validity for our entry could be constantly present in the minds of all the negotiators.

THE ALTERNATIVES

When thinking about these reasons we should also at this point perhaps consider what the alternatives confronting this country are likely to be if for one reason or another we cannot join the EEC. One broad alternative of course would be for us to get ever nearer to the USA and perhaps eventually end up with some kind of merger. Again in a general way, and in the long run, this is perhaps the most likely solution though not, I would submit, the best. There is a common language, there is, as we have seen in a previous chapter, a considerable common history. The same applies to a larger extent to the so-called 'Old Dominions' and notably to Australia and New Zealand and to a large extent Canada as well. In the course of time, there is little reason to suppose that some kind of Anglo-Saxon *bloc* might not be achieved of which the centre of gravity would of course be Washington. Nor is there any reason why such a *bloc* could not enter into a reasonably satisfactory relationship with the African and Asian members of the Commonwealth, though it is true that the more evident it became that the capital of the *bloc* was in Washington the less likelihood would there be of running the Commonwealth on its present lines as a sort of friendly multiracial club.

A variant of such a loose Anglo-Saxon confederation would be for the United Kingdom and Canada and perhaps even Australasia as well actually to join the United States, or at any rate to enter into a definite union, whose seat, if not in Washington, would almost certainly have to be somewhere in the New World. This would seem to be less likely than the first alternative, if only for the fact that it is difficult to see all the other Anglo-Saxons being welcomed as fellow citizens by the United States Congress. The first alternative therefore remains a distinct possibility, if not a probability, and it is even conceivable, supposing the EEC breaks up that a number of northern European states might also one day join the grouping.

The real disadvantage of such a makeshift solution would be not that we should (as de Gaulle says) 'lose our national identity' but that it could in no wise solve the basic problems of the Western Alliance. Even if the Scandinavian states were not associated with the Anglo-Saxon group, but rather made their peace with the Common Market, which is perhaps unlikely, it is difficult to see how the latter could survive, given the political strains to which it would be subjected. Attempts to create a 'Third Force' in Europe without Britain would almost certainly fail: the last thing the Germans would want in the circumstances would be the withdrawal of the American Army. So would a more healthy tendency towards creating some kind of autonomous Western Europe within the framework of the Alliance, if only for the fact that such a body could only be based on French hegemony which, in the continued presence of American troops, would clearly be impossible, and in their absence would no doubt be more impossible still. On the other hand, if the EEC did break up for one reason or another, the situation could hardly be satisfactory. For the French and other Europeans would be unlikely to accommodate themselves to the complete American economic and political hegemony which would then be the sole alternative, and might prefer to have governments which in one way or another, would be likely to seek special arrangements with the Soviet Union.

There is theoretically, one other possible alternative. It is conceivable that in between America and some enlarged EEC, Britain might decided to disarm completely and seek to enter into friendly and economic and political relations with the bulk of the countries of the 'Third World'. Since she might as a disarmed nation be expected to compete with her larger rivals and even to build up her reserves which in the absence of armaments would chiefly be used for the purposes of aid, this might seem to some to be an attractive solution, more especially perhaps if it were combined with a fairly closely directed economy thus achieving what might be called socialism in our time. This might be the hope, but it could also well be that such a neutrality, based as it would be on a very small home market, would result in a decline in the standard of living in Britain. It would not be at all possible to defend what used to be considered British interests in any part of the world. Few people would favour this solution now but in the event of some severe economic crisis, it might well be that a good many would favour it. What seems quite certain is that none of these solutions is on any showing so alluring as that of joining a prosperous EEC as an equal with the other great European states, and putting our unique experience both in the sphere of administration and in that of parliament at the disposal of our neighbours.

Finally, it might be said that on the perhaps unlikely assumption that the EEC breaks up, we could work for some kind of confederal free trade Europe which would be definitely under our leadership. The great difficulty here would be to get back effectively to the early post-war system whereby we did manage to assert a leadership on this basis in Western Europe. It also seems quite probable that if the EEC did break up the economic results would be extremely painful and it is quite possible that in these circumstances either France or Germany, or more likely perhaps, Italy would try to make her peace with the Soviet Union rather than with America and establish some 'Yugoslav' or, more typically perhaps, 'Rumanian' régime. We can well imagine the effect in this country of any such development.

There is no doubt, in other words, that when examined closely all the alternatives to our joining the EEC – always supposing that it continues to exist – are a great deal less attractive than British membership of the Community. If reason, and not emotion, can be our guide, the balance of advantage clearly points in one direction. There are still outstanding matters which can only be settled by negotiations carried on an atmosphere of goodwill. It will still be necessary for this country to accept willingly some supra-national features. What these are will now be discussed. For it is no good saying we want to join the EEC unless we realize what precisely we shall be in for.

CHAPTER EIGHT

*

How Would Entry Affect Britain?

LET us suppose that the will to create a Community exists on both sides of the Channel: that negotiations have succeeded in ironing out the economic difficulties (disposal of the agricultural levies, transitional periods, voting formula, EFTA agreement, etc.) in the way of Britain joining the EEC; that the political structure of the Six has not yet finally been established but remains an essential objective to which Britain, if she comes in, will be obliged to subscribe; that the EEC remains in existence as a necessary precondition to all this. How far would entry then be acceptable to the British and what exactly would be involved economically, socially and politically if we did go in?

We have seen how the EEC itself works or is intended to work and we must assume for the purpose of the present argument that its progress in accordance with the procedure laid down in the Treaty is not seriously disrupted. There is nothing in the functioning of this machine which should alarm us. Certain decisions affecting our economy would, it is perfectly true, from the start be taken elsewhere than in Westminster; but they would be decisions which would first of all have been prepared by a body of independent European experts which would include British members, then arrived at by a Council of Ministers in which it would be very difficult, to say the least, for us to be overruled even in the unlikely event of a majority of our colleagues siding against us on any particular issue, and finally subjected to the scrutiny of a European Parliament in which we should have a great say and where our excellent parliamentarians would probably be able to play a major rôle. Why should such a régime be considered to be more derogatory to national sentiment than any other? After all, even now we are largely at the mercy of decisions taken in bodies such as the International Monetary Fund (which acts by means of a qualified majority vote) or the so-called Group of Ten. Even a Labour Government has been unable to ignore the opinions of the international bankers. Matters which affect directly every man, woman and child in these islands, including the nuclear defence of the West, are even now being decided for us largely by foreigners. Even in bodies where the unanimity rule officially prevails it may well be that a large majority will decide on a certain course and in practice all we can do is to register our disapproval by an abstention. In a word, the whole world is, in a sense becoming increasingly one and we cannot now remain wholly independent, even if we should wish to do so. The EEC, if we should come into it would thus be essentially a means of settling certain economic questions in a manner satisfactory both to us and to our nearest neighbours. There is no doubt that, provided there is a reasonable weighted voting formula and certain preliminary difficulties are settled equitably, it could work out, as indeed it is now working out among the Six, to the general advantage, and in no sense to the detriment of any particular member.

It is quite true that in certain delicate spheres, such as immigration, we should no doubt be under an obligation to consult with out partners; but there would be no obligation on us to restrict or encourage immigrants. Germany was at perfect liberty to continue to import millions of workers from Eastern Germany and France hundreds of thousands from Italy and Algeria. Under the Treaty of Rome we could certainly go on importing many thousand coloured immigrants from the Commonwealth as well as (for example) Italians if we so preferred. In the course of time it is obvious that some kind of understanding as regards immigration into the whole Community ought to be arrived at in the interests of all. In the course of time too we should eventually arrive at a state in which a common immigration policy will have to be adopted for the whole group, just as it is in the United States: but not until all are agreed that this is necessary and desirable.

There are many other fields in which this gradual approach would be adopted, and there is no reason whatever to be disturbed by the possible consequences for the people of Britain if it is. It is rather what may happen to our people if we do not join some larger group that ought to be worrying us now. Unable to afford to be a Great Power, unwilling and perhaps unable too to be a small neutral power like Switzerland or Sweden, we shall be increasingly at the mercy of events, and the disciplines to which we should perforce have to subject outselves would be likely to be much more unpleasant than any which we should have to accept as a full member of the EEC.

Having grasped this we must nevertheless realize that there are other directions in which we should also have to come together gradually with out neighbours. Our criminal law and our magnificient system whereby justice is not only done but is seen to be done would be in no wise affected, but in some spheres it is obvious that an approximation of the various legal systems should be attempted. Company law might with great advantage be brought into harmony over the entire area as would the provisions relating to monopolies. Then certainly taxation would have to be gradually equalized – a very difficult, but not an impossible task. It would be wrong that one member of the Community should bear burdens proportionally far greater than another. Nor would it be desirable, if capital could flow without let or hindrance throughout the area, that it should be penalized in one country more than another. Finally an effort would undoubtedly be made to equalize social benefits and to harmonize social legislation generally. In some countries of the Six they are higher than in Britain, in others lower. This is already being done to some extent under the aegis of the Council of Europe. There is no reason why there should not be a general increase in social benefits following on the great economies that would be effected as a result of a pooling of armaments. But all this would be a very gradual process. In a general way it might legitimately be hoped that public opinion in Britain would find the economic implications of the Treaty of Rome as outlined above entirely acceptable. But it remains to consider the perhaps more difficult question of what the foreign and defence implications would be if we joined the Common Market.

That there must be some political content is fairly obvious. In the EEC itself there comes a moment, and it will no doubt be reached before we come in ourselves, when the system of majority voting on major issue comes into operation and when it is in any case necessary to take certain fairly far-reaching political decisions such as whether and how to complete the economic as opposed to the customs union, and whether it is really possible to decide on such important matters as the disposal of the proceeds of the agricultural levies without the approval of a Parliament more representative of the peoples of the Six than the present nominated Assembly at Strasbourg. But all such political element is something that must, if the EEC endures, be produced by the very force of things. You cannot have a full blown economic union – and that is the declared intention of the Community – without the equivalent of a common currency. And a common currency is scarcely conceivable without a common central system of reserves, which in its turn is not conceivable without an authority of some kind on which it will depend. It is useless to think therefore that if we do come into the EEC, we shall not be heading towards some kind of European, or rather Western European authority. We shall. This process might be held up; it is indeed at present being held up by the Gaullist government of France; but it cannot indefinitely be held up without the collapse of the EEC and a reversion to that economic and political nationalism which is the only conceivable alternative.

What is especially important here, however, is to consider before we come into a Community of this nature what effect this would have on our country in what is still the absolute preserve of the nation-state, namely, foreign policy and defence. Would there be any prospect, to put the problem in a nutshell, of our ever being forced against our will, to declare war, adopt conscription, dissolve our Foreign Service, or put the armed forces of HM The Queen into some kind of international uniform, or even subject Her Majesty herself to the overriding authority of a President of Europe? The answer is emphatically, no. Such things, if they ever come about would only come about by common consent among the members of the Community. It is true that by the time the economic union has been achieved and we have a common agricultural, transport, energy and social policy, to say nothing of a common currency, it may well seem absurd not to have a method of arriving at common decisions in the field of foreign policy and defence, also, more especially if steps have already been taken in the direction of achieving this. We should therefore be well-advised to consider here and now what sort of Political and Defence Community we should be prepared to enter into on the assumptions (*a*) that this had not yet been decided on by the Six and (*b*) that minimum machinery of some kind would nevertheless be absolutely necessary in a Community which had reached the point of taking certain decisions by a qualified majority vote, even if it had not yet arrived at the stage of full, or even partial economic union. Here is a field in which we might indeed take the initiative by putting forward some scheme that might appeal to all who believe in the construction of some real European unity whether they are in favour of going fast or slowly towards the agreed objective.

If we had joined the EEC in 1963 it is indeed possible that some Political and Defence Community might by this time, and with our own consent, have grown out of the EEC machinery itself, but this did not happen. It would probably still be open to us, however, if we so desired, to suggest the broad lines of some new Political and Defence Community which might be established even before we enter the EEC though naturally it would be preferable for the two events to coincide if possible. We should therefore first look at the problem from a general point of view and see whether there is any solution which we could *not* accept, that is to say a solution which, if it were insisted on by the Six, would actually prevent us from joining any Political and Defence Association and hence *a priori* from joining the Common Market. We can say at once that there is indeed one such eventuality. If the Six were to agree on a military and political structure which was, or was intended to be, quite untied to America, in other words a 'Third Force', as the saying goes, then we could not join, even if staying out might have all the serious consequences to which reference has already been made. For such a solution would clearly postulate the prompt withdrawal of United States troops from Germany and by that very act the probable withdrawal of the American nuclear 'umbrella' over Western Europe without its replacement by a joint Atlantic defence system. The idea that for a long time at any rate our security in our small peninsula could be assured by some combination of the British and French *Forces de Frappe* only is not one which would appeal to many people in Britain, even if it did have a considerable appeal in France. It would of course, have even less appeal in Germany from which country the Americans for their part are not likely to be pushed out if they can help it. We may therefore safely conclude that, whatever may happen in the future, a 'Third Force' solution is not politically practicable now. Insistence by the French on such a theory could prevent any Political and Defence Community from being formed, whether we were parties to it or not. Here therefore we are concerned with the kind of Community which Britain might agree to join and which would have some chance of being constructed in the near future with British participation. What sort of thing could this be?

It would have to be something, clearly, which was both inside the Western Alliance and nevertheless an entity of its own. If it is to be inside the Alliance it cannot, for so long as the Americans are in Europe, have the power to pursue a policy, or to take military decisions regarding Europe against the Americans' will. In particular it should not have any right to threaten the use of nuclear power without the consent of America or indeed to indulge in serious negotiations with the adversary without their knowledge and approval. For if it did there would be two authorities within the Alliance which might quite well be at loggerheads. And in such circumstances the Alliance would, of course, promptly collapse; in other words a 'Third Force' policy is simply not consonant with the maintenance of the Alliance. But equally if the EEC continues on its appointed path it will surely before long become some sort of political as well as an economic animal. And if it does become some such animal then it will undoubtedly have a will of its own and be able, if necessary, to disagree with US policy to the extent at any rate of obliging the Americans to take some common European view into account in (for instance) the conduct of their Asian policies. Consequently it looks as if our Political and Defence Community must at once have the power of arriving somehow at common decisions and possess, if not complete independence – what entity except the super-state now possesses *complete* independence? – at any rate a reasonable degree of autonomy. Thus it would certainly have to be agreed, for a start, that whereas the European Political and Defence Community would not be able to have an independent nuclear policy, so the USA would not be able to ignore the advice of a United Europe. In other words, for so long as there was an American military presence in a United Europe the Alliance could only function on the basis of what is technically called a 'double veto'. There could therefore be no question of either the British or the French deterrents being employed or threatened individually, nor could there be any question, for so long as the American Army is in Germany, of their being used collectively without American consent. Equally the Americans would have to agree not to deploy their own nuclear arm in Europe without the consent, at the outset of Britain and France, and, as soon as possible, of the European Political and Defence Community. This would be the essential basis for any British participation in the European Political and Defence Community. On this rock we must build up our general scheme.

It should be noted at once that though such a system would be quite incompatible with the concept of a totally independent 'Third Force', it would be compatible with the original suggestion of President Kennedy, namely, that the Alliance should rest on 'two pillars', one in the East and one in the West, and that, gradually, machinery should be established for constructing, as it were, an arch between the two pillars. On this assumption, the essential preliminary machinery for the European pillar would obviously have to be a Council of Ministers, who might even from the start take certain decisions by the same qualified majority vote as would apply in the economic sphere, e.g. in the sphere of the standardization of armaments, where the unanimity rule at present prevents any progress being made at all whether in NATO or in a Western European Union. It could further be agreed, in principle, that as confidence grows, so this system of qualified majority voting could be extended to other spheres in the realm of foreign policy and defence, and eventually that all decisions will be taken by such means, even in the crucial nuclear sphere. (The button will never be pressed, but it is psychologically of the first importance to know who, in theory, will press the button.) To assist the Council there should clearly also be an independent commission modelled on the Commission of the EEC, the functions of which we have already examined. All that would be necessary to start off with would be to agree that members of this political commission (which might also deal with defence matters) should be men of much standing in their respective countries and in the confidence of their own governments, appointed by the member states, acting in unanimity, for a period of years. It should be established that the Council should refer to this body all important matters on which there appeared to be a division of view among the governments with the purpose, if possible, of arriving at some common policy which might then be recommended to the Ministers themselves. All the members of the commission would of course be under an obligation to receive no instructions from their governments and to consider all problems submitted to them from a purely European as opposed to a purely national point of view. The chairman of this body, which could take its decisions by simple majority vote, should sit with the Council of Ministers as an equal though naturally without the right to vote. His duty would be constantly to encourage them to arrive at a common view in all matters relating to foreign policy and defence. Other members of the commission would no doubt also be present at Council meetings.

It would thus be for this body, as I see it, to prepare schemes for close European co-operation in the defence of the Free World generally. For instance British strategy in South-East Asia, and indeed in the Indian Ocean area, should first be cleared with our colleagues and some joint plan should be devised for putting it into effect. It would presumably be some time before any joint European peace-keeping force could be devised; and pending its achievement it would no doubt be France or Britain who would actually be responsible for the conduct of any operations, whether in Asia or Africa. But common financing ought certainly to be arranged and at least a concerted policy should be achievable. What is important is that the common interest of Europe in any particular problem should always be identified, and once this is done it should be the duty of the spokesman for Europe in the NATO Council to try to co-ordinate it with the policy of the United States. In this joint policy-forming process there are many organizations which could help, the Atlantic Treaty Association (with its powerful component of the Atlantic Council of the United States), the Atlantic Institute, and indeed the NATO Parliamentarians themselves, to mention only a few. In these bodies, and elsewhere, a great dialogue between the two sides of the Atlantic should be perpetually conducted with the object of reconciling ends and means, and if possible arriving at a common Western viewpoint. Needless to say, disarmament too should enter into such discussions, and into the deliberations of the Commission, if only for the fact that serious disagreement between the members of the European Community on such matters as proliferation of nuclear weapons would not be consonant with the maintenance of the Community itself.

It cannot be repeated too often that the establishment of such a commission would be the thing most likely to encourage the sentiment of European solidarity and the eventual formation of some agreed policy even in the most difficult and contentious spheres. For once this system is introduced and begins to function the monopoly of the national Foreign Ministers and Ministers of Defence is broken and the mystique of the nation-state disappears. No longer would Britain and France be thinking entirely in terms of self-sufficiency and 'balanced' armaments. They would be obliged to consider the interests of the entire group. Apart indeed from certain categories of questions which would from the start by agreement be subject if necessary to some majority decision in the Council, none of the other provisions would in any way limit the 'sovereignty' of the component nations but would merely facilitate the gradual emergence of a common will.

Finally, it would be agreed that the European Parliament – in which all member nations should be represented roughly on a population basis – should have the right at least to discuss and to make recommendations regarding the foreign policy and defence matters which would be submitted to the Political and Defence Commission for independent study. Within the limits of security, members of the commission as well as Ministers should be interrogated by the committees of this Parliament. The point at which the Parliament should be directly elected should, as in the Treaty of Rome, be effectively put off until there is unanimity among the member nations, or at any rate among the major states, for such a development. The essential thing, however, would be that, from the start, there would be some kind of democratic control over the operations of the Political and Defence Community, just as there is such control at present over the operations in this sphere of individual nation states.

There is no doubt that some system as I have just described would not be acceptable to the present government of France, but it would certainly be acceptable to the other present governments of the Six, and if it were actually put forward by Her Majesty's Government – perhaps at some meeting of the Western European Union – it would have a tremendous effect in Europe. If it did nothing else it would probably prevent the formation of some kind of political union which, even if not exactly a 'Third Force', would be rather anti-American in tendency and more inclined in fact, if not in name, to resemble the well-known *Europe des Etats*, which, as we have assumed before, can only function if there is a hegemony on the part of one of the states-members, and notably of France.

In any case the broad scheme for an economic, political and defence union suggested in this chapter would not resemble a unitary state: would be considerably less than a federation in the usually accepted sense of the word; and yet would be much more than a simple alliance or an unworkable *Europe des Etats*. If we say that we are 'Europeans' at all, it is difficult to see how we can fail to go at least as far as I have suggested. He who wills an economic end, that is to say he who wants for obvious economic reasons our full participation in a European market, must also will the political means. Nor is there the slightest reason to suppose that such a system, which would be an entirely novel one from the point of view of international relations, would result in any loss of national identity, of *diminutio capitis*, or the feeling that we were as a nation something less than we were before. None of our great traditions or institutions would be challenged. No one would feel that he was at the mercy of the foreigner or that Britain was inevitably getting the muddy end of the stick. Fnally, no one should imagine that such a system, provided there were satisfactory arrangements, even if only of a provisional character, for Commonwealth trade, would result in any weakening of the Commonwealth connection, and this requires a few paragraphs of explanation itself.

The Commonwealth, as we all know, is not an economic or even a political entity. It is of great value as a multiracial club which is, however, a very different thing. So far as trade is concerned, whatever the recent lamentations, the fact is that all members of the Commonwealth are tending to trade more with nations other than the metropolis than they did before, and this, from the point of view of the world generally, is a very good thing. It is excellent for instance that Japan should import more and more meat and dairy produce from Australasia and New Zealand, if only for the reason that were this impossible, forces might gather strength in Japan as they did in the twenties and thirties which might once again produce a political explosion or more likely, perhaps, a close association with the Communist Chinese. It is also a fact that the accumulation of agricultural surpluses is a worldwide problem which must be dealt with by commodity agreements or otherwise: it cannot possibly be considered in the sole context of Commonwealth trade. Finally, it is a fact that many of the interests of Commonwealth countries are opposed and not identical and that the Commonwealth is simply not comparable to some superpower or even to such a body as the EEC is to lose all touch with reality. It must be added that, as has been repeatedly said, Britain cannot conceivably by itself supply the vast capital sums which are necessary if the underdeveloped countries of the Commonwealth are to be developed, and that in any case such aid ought to be co-ordinated not only with that of America but with that of European countries as well.

Hence the entry of Britain into some kind of European Union of the type suggested would in no way prejudice relations between Britain and the Commonwealth; it would facilitate them to a remarkable degree. There is no reason whatever why, if Britain is a member of the European Community, Commonwealth conferences should not take place from time to time in London as they do today. It would be most useful for Britain to be able to represent the views of many Commonwealth countries – for they surely would not be unanimous – in the European Council of Ministers when efforts are made to arrive at a common European point of view. There is no reason why the European Community as a whole should not take over from Britain the task of arranging and encouraging Commonwealth development. It is true that Britain, if only because of the fact that English is a common language, would probably have to take the lead in this respect in the European sphere, but at the moment Britain is quite incapable of meeting the educational needs of a Commonwealth of seven hundred million people, and the more Commonwealth students are able to go to France, Germany, Italy, Holland and elsewhere the better it will clearly be for the interests of all. The great thing is that the developing Commonwealth countries should regard Europe, including Britain, not as a 'neo-colonialist' but as a real partner in the gigantic process of the industrialization of the world. The image of the old type of colonialist with his solar topee and his sjambok has happily been shattered: that of the neo-colonialist must now be changed and the formation of a United Europe is the way to change it.

All these things ought to be explained to the British people by a Government determined, if it can, to bring this country into the twentieth century and also to perpetuate, and not lose, that still extensive influence in the world that our fathers and grandfathers have left us.

CHAPTER NINE

*

The Partnership

LET us be optimistic. Let us suppose that a Britain, conscious of her new destiny, succeeds in an effort to establish with her neighbours a European Political and Defence Community designed, not as a rival to America, but as part and parcel of the Western world. Indeed unless we do make this supposition it is useless to say that we want to 'come into Europe' in the sense of joining the EEC, which if it is anything, is a political affair, and we had better concentrate on making the best of one of the alternatives mentioned in Chapter Seven. On the assumption made, however, we must certainly have some idea of how a continuing Western Alliance might be expected to work and what the prospects would then be of forming what is commonly if sometimes rather misleadingly known as 'the Atlantic Community'.

As we have already noted, the conception of a 'partnership' between America and a United Europe was first put forward by President Kennedy in 1962. It was of course based on the erroneous assumption that Britain would shortly be in the Common Market and that some kind of Western European political authority would at least be on the horizon, even if it were many years before it appeared in any very concrete form. The Alliance, therefore, as the late President saw it, would henceforward rest on two pillars, one in the East and one in the West and an equal partnership would be created between the two whereby the problems confronting the Western world would be worked out together and an effort would be made

111

to share burdens and to arrive, if possible, at a common foreign, or at any rate a common Cold War policy. This splendid idea should surely have encouraged all the Europeans to abandon any suspicions that the United States was seeking to dominate her allies, or impose any kind of veiled hegemony. America was actually begging them to become an equal in every way, on one sole condition, namely, that they should come together and try to work out a common policy of their own – even a common nuclear policy – which could then be approximated to that of America. In the event, Britain's application to join the EEC was rejected; President Kennedy was assassinated; and the partnership idea has for the last three years been in cold storage. This does not mean that it is dead, because in the long run as I believe it is still the only satisfactory solution.

There are of course already in existence certain 'Atlantic' institutions which would obviously have to be used for the purpose of putting any partnership into effect. They are the NATO Council itself, the Organization for Economic Co-operation and Development in Paris and the NATO Parliamentarians. The first two are governmental bodies in which the unanimity rule applies, the last is at the moment a largely unofficial gathering with no statutory powers. How might they work, supposing that the EEC were enlarged to include the United Kingdom, Denmark, Norway, Ireland, with the other present members of EFTA entering into some kind of association with the EEC?

Let us take the NATO Council first. On our assumption, namely, that some European Political and Defence Community has been established which is beginning to reach its own decisions, anyhow in certain spheres, it will be clear that nine members of the NATO Council out of fifteen would have created what in effect would be a special group in the Council, which would presumably often, in a preliminary way, consider certain matters before the Council did so itself. Up to now such a procedure has not been officially countenanced by the Council, but it is true that the United States, the United Kingdom and France form a special body known as the 'Standing

Group' in Washington and that Germany is to some extent associated with this group. Supposing that European members of the Council, or some of them, had by the nature of things to consider certain local aspects of European defence by themselves, they could if they wished form a special group in that Council for that purpose. In any case, if they do, for the reasons stated earlier in this book, form some kind of Defence Community (and after all no Political Community can in practice be divorced from Defence), it is clear that they would somehow have to express a common view on certain defence problems in the NATO Council. What therefore would seem the best plan would be for the European body, whatever it may be, to form part of a reorganized NATO machine including the Americans and the other allies and it would then be the principal function of NATO to work out some common policy for the Alliance as a whole and to have the last word on general strategy. Since Turkey, Greece and Portugal will almost certainly, if Britain, Norway and Denmark join the EEC, become associates of that body in so far as they are not associates already, there is no particular reason why they themselves should not also join the European Political and Defence Community as associates. The neutrals (associates we should hope of the EEC), namely, Sweden, Austria, Switzerland, and perhaps also Ireland, would clearly have to stay outside, though Ireland, as a prospective member of the EEC, would of course have the right to come into the Political and Defence Community if she wanted to. If all this were done, the establishment within the framework of the Alliance of some common policy for the Alliance might well be a more simple process than it is now.

All such arrangements would in practice have to be considered in relation to the reform of NATO itself since, though the Treaty does not end in 1969 it nevertheless then becomes open for any member state to resign from the Organization if it wishes. The suggestion has also been made that it would be desirable to create in NATO something equivalent to a political commission for the whole Alliance. The real difficulty here is that whereas such a proposal makes sense when the commission is serving a body which in the last resort makes up its mind by some kind of qualified majority, it is very difficult to employ a commission when the body, as in the case of NATO, acts by unanimity. It is even more difficult to adopt the techniques when there is one superior power, even if some of the others come together in a Community. Nevertheless assuming that the Secretary-General of NATO can by agreement, have rather more powers than at present, it might be possible for him to have the closest relations with the European Political and Defence Commission with the object of preparing the broad lines of various policies that might be adopted to bring the aims and objectives of both partners into harmony. This indeed might be the principal preoccupation of a reformed Secretariat.

The same techniques might, broadly speaking, apply in OECD. Here we have a much larger body than the NATO Council consisting of all the European states this side of the Iron Curtain, plus the United States and Canada, the whole in association with Japan. In the economic sphere the Six are now beginning to talk with one voice and have indeed reached the point at which negotiations on behalf of the whole group in the Kennedy Round are being officially conducted by the Commission in Brussels. If this process should really take root and on the assumption that the present applicants join the EEC, the main object of OECD would be to achieve the harmonization of European, North American and Japanese economic policies. So far as the actual partnership goes, we could either think in terms of the appointment of some small European/American group within the framework of OECD itself, or we might contemplate giving increased powers to the present Secretary-General and his officials.

For their part, the NATO Parliamentarians have obviously the possibility of developing into a real Atlantic Assembly. In the event of any partnership being established it is indeed essential that they should be so transformed. The Assembly would then have to possess certain real but limited powers and function on much the same lines as the Parliament of Europe in Strasbourg. Ideally it would consist of representatives from the

European NATO countries and North America in roughly
equal proportions. Whether the European neutrals should participate would be a matter for debate. Presumably they would
not feel able to take part in any voting, but they might well
welcome being present as observers. It would, however, be
apparent that for such time as the unanimity rule had to apply
in the other organs of the incipient Atlantic Community, the
Atlantic Assembly could not fulfil such an important rôle as
that fulfilled by the Parliament of Europe. The partnership, if
formed, would indeed tend towards the construction of such
a Community, but it would be a slower business even than the
construction of Europe. In any case the general conception of
the partnership would be more likely to result eventually in
some genuine Atlantic Community than anything else. Indeed
short of an Atlantic Federation, or a generally accepted
American hegemony it is difficult to imagine any other basis on
which it could possibly be constructed.

In all discussion of an Atlantic Community it is important to
define the end precisely and to try to arrive at preliminary agreement as to that. If Western Europe is ever formed, then the
Atlantic Community could only rest on the arch connecting the
two pillars – in fact it would be the arch, and we have sought
to show how this could be constructed. In principle then, the
Community should be composed of two entities, with Canada
performing some special rôle (which we will come to immediately) and the Atlantic Assembly constantly examining proposals for reinforcing the arch. Other states which for political
or other reasons could not actually join one of these entities
should be associates. There might be eight of them in Europe
and one (Japan) in the Far East. In the event of a German settlement there might be even more in Eastern Europe. Efforts
should, however, certainly be made not to enlarge the European pillar unduly. If it is to cohere, it must do so slowly and
this process would certainly be prejudiced if too many states
came in too soon as full members, or even as associates. But the
important thing to remember is that if there is no European
pillar then there simply cannot be an arch.

Supposing indeed that Europe is not formed, in other words supposing the EEC either dissolves or does not make any further progress, supposing even that it does make progress but that Europe still remains divided into two, any alternative Atlantic machinery would necessarily be dominated by the vote of America, unless a unitary state were formed or the unanimity rule were rigorously preserved, in which last case there would be no real progress beyond the maintenance of the present rather inadequate machinery. Whatever scheme therefore we may personally favour we must admit two things if some meaningful Atlantic partnership is really going to be formed: (*a*) some kind of Western European Political Community must first be created and begin to function, however inadequately, and (*b*) all machinery for developing further the Alliance or the Community as a whole will be still a matter depending on what action happens in the development of a United Western Europe. There is, however, one difficulty in the way of creating any institutions based in theory on the two pillars. That is the position of Canada. This is something which should be faced and if possible tackled from the outset.

Canadians rightly draw attention to the fact that they have not been told either by President Kennedy or anyone else how they would fit in to any partnership system. Therefore at the moment they tend rather to favour some reform of NATO which would give more influence to the small and medium powers. When I was in Ottawa in September 1964, I did, however, make a suggestion which I trust may be considered when and if Britain joins the EEC. It seemed to me that, more especially as she is a bi-racial country, there would be a considerable case for placing 'Atlantic' institutions in Canada, and notably perhaps in Montreal and Quebec. So far as NATO is concerned, it might well be that the military machine, i.e. SHAPE, would have to remain in Paris, or if that is not desired then elsewhere in Europe, but part of the machinery could no doubt be situated in Canada, and certainly the OECD could be transported to Montreal without any particular difficulty. In any case, the NATO Parliamentarians might well have their centre in Montreal. If this body should ever become institutionalized, then it would certainly have to have a centre somewhere just as the Parliament of Europe is situated in Strasbourg, and Montreal from many points of view would seem to be indicated for this purpose. As it seems to me such a development should go far to satisfy the desire of Canada to play a distinctive rôle in the Alliance. It might well be also that when representatives of a United Europe eventually meet representatives of the United States in Montreal within the framework of the Alliance, they might sometimes do well to arrange for a Canadian chairman.

This therefore would be the general way in which some partnership might be expected to work but, in practice, whatever progress is made towards achieving a European Union, Western Europe will not for many years be actually represented by one person in the Councils of the Alliance. In the NATO Council, in the NATO Parliamentarians, even in OECD, I should be inclined to bet that it will not be before 1975 that there is a card in front of one of the participants marked 'Europe' or 'Western Europe'. When it comes therefore to a common Western European view already arrived at in some European Political and Defence Community being expressed in, for example, the NATO Council, it will no doubt be expressed by arrangement, by one of the Community's component powers. This would no doubt not be ideal from the American point of view, but no system is likely to be ideal, and in any case we must start from the assumption that, whether we like it or not, some entity will probably be created in Western Europe which will eventually have its own representatives.

In any case, for so long as the American Army remains in Germany and successful efforts are made by one means or another to create a unified, or a partially unified, Western Europe the partnership remains the only conceivable method of regulating the affairs of the West. If the presence of American troops in Germany is still contemplated and the EEC does not produce any political element and is not extended, then admittedly no formal partnership will be necessary. The United

States would presumably deal separately with its allies in the general framework of some NATO Council. If the American Army in Germany were withdrawn it would still be necessary, presumably, to employ partnership techniques of some kind for so long as the Western Alliance remained – which might not be long in the circumstances – unless indeed by that time Europe had developed enough strength to ensure, at any rate partially, its own defence, and even then it would still be highly desirable to have some kind of partnership machinery.

It remains to consider what effect any partnership is likely to have on the prospects of coming to some arrangement with the Russians as regards Eastern Europe generally, and notably as regards the reunification of Germany. So long as the American Army remains in Germany the prospects of arriving at any permanent East–West settlement are admittedly not great. But it is devoutly to be hoped that the American Army will nevertheless remain in Germany until such time as the Russians are prepared to contemplate some scheme for the reunification of the Germans which does not result in a reunified Reich being either neutralized or coming under Soviet domination. This will not prevent good relations between the West and the states of Eastern Europe, it will not even prevent some kind of 'special relationship' between the Federal Republic and the Deutsche Demokratische Republik. On the other hand, if there is no partnership that is to say if America does not have the benefit of any collective European advice, it is possible that East–West tension may exist for longer than is at present thought probable. What is certain is that concentration in 'Atlantic' circles on some kind of 'Wider Europe', which might be brought into existence before Britain joins the EEC, if she ever does, is quite unrealistic. Nobody disputes the effect that good relations with Eastern Europe are desirable, but from a political point of view the admission of such states, even as associates, to either the present or an enlarged EEC would only be possible in the event of some prior major agreement between the United States and the Soviet Union about the future of Germany.

To sum up this chapter, the partnership remains the only

reasonable objective both for Western Europeans and for North Americans. Progress towards achieving it (though it must continuously be made) cannot, however, be rapid until such time as an effective Western Europe has been established, including the United Kingdom. In the meantime, the Alliance can only carry on on the basis of an implicit American leadership. If a European Political and Defence Community is formed it would be for that body gradually to establish its own relationship with America within the framework of the Alliance.

CHAPTER TEN

*

A Theory of Regionalism

THE present world system is still largely bi-polar but the political Ice Age that followed the war is breaking up. China is already advancing on to the scene as a third centre of power: it seems possible that India may one day constitute another, more particularly if, in spite of present difficulties, any loose association with Pakistan can ever come about. If Western Europe is formed with the accession of Britain it will not be a Third Force for so long as American troops are in Germany; but if there is a subsequent German settlement involving a joint Russo-American withdrawal then indeed it could be one, though by that time the phrase will probably be irrelevant, since in the circumstances a 'climate of peace' would no doubt extend eastwards from Fairbanks, Alaska, to Vladivostok. It seems unlikely, therefore, that either India or a new Europe would go in for an enormous nuclear programme – though in default of general disarmament both might have certain nuclear arms. But politically, they would clearly speak with increasing authority in the great councils of the world. How far could such a regional system spread, and is there reason to suppose that it could be the base for a new World Authority, replacing the present rather powerless United Nations, and thus ending the dangerous international anarchy of our age?

There are those who say that all such ideas are the purest 'globaloney'; that even if you ever did get these huge blocs into existence, or some of them, the first thing they would do would be to fall out and fight a global war: that, far from seeking to create new giants, the best thing would be to try to reduce the excessive power of the present ones, leaving 130 nation-states or so to work out unaided their own destinies, God for us all, as I have already quoted, and the devil take the hindmost. Alliances might be formed, of course, but they would not necessarily be enduring. Eventually some kind of balance might be arrived at though maybe as the result of continuing conventional wars, nuclear escalation being avoided by mutual terror. This would no doubt seem sensible to the nationalist mind, and indeed it may well prove to be our future. But apart from its desirability, or otherwise, the theory seems to take little account of the unifying forces of modern technology and the pressures which are being increasingly exerted on the totally independent nation-state.

As against such 'realistic' forecasts and desire to 'let nature take her course' we have idealists who say that we should arrange some vast new social contract, all the 130 nation-states varying in size from China to Luxembourg agreeing to enter into a World Parliament in which each would cast votes proportionate to its size and power, e.g. China, 3,500 or so and Luxembourg 1. This 'Parliament of Man' could no doubt form a World Executive, irrespective of national ties and the World Executive would elect a World President. There would be one World Police Force under the Executive. One World Court would administer justice. One language, perhaps English, would be adopted by mutual agreement. It would all be the triumph of reason, the final achievement of the Tennysonian proposal for a Federation of the World.

It seems to me that neither the one vision of the triumph of nationalism nor the other of World Federation can be shared by those who regard the future with comparatively open eyes. The fact is that Regions are appearing in the modern world and we must accept the fact that this is a tendency which is likely to continue. Thus China has already established herself as a new centre of attraction. India may not have done so yet, but there is now some reason to suppose that she may get the better of her population problem in which case economic progress should be rapid. Whether she will be a nuclear power is open to doubt. She could be if she so desired. Perhaps some 'token' nuclear capability is the answer for India and perhaps for one or two other states as well. Such limited 'proliferation' would not be the worst of the dangers which confront us at the present time.

In any case, the whole purpose of this book is to suggest that, in spite of nationalistic urges, the chances still are that some valid European Union, including Britain, will eventually emerge. It is true that neither the emergence of a United Europe as a world force nor that of a 'Greater India' is certain; but on a balance of probability both would seem to be on the cards. Assuming therefore that, shall we say, by 1984 you have not two or three 'poles of authority', as at present, but five, what chances are there if other 'Regions' achieving some similar status and thus avoiding undue tension by making it difficult, or impossible, for any one centre to advance its own individual interests and its area of influence with a view to achieving an empire, or in other words, the mastery of the world?

The areas concerned are obviously South America, the Middle East, South-East Asia and Africa south of the Sahara. All these are already recognized as Regions in a preliminary and no doubt quite inadequate way. Latin America already forms a separate group in the United Nations and in the Organization of American States it is intimately linked, as it should be, with, the United States, in the same sort of way as the latter is and, it is to be hoped, will continue to be linked to Europe through the machine of the Western Alliance, and ultimately, no doubt, through the constitution of some 'Atlantic' Community. Can we imagine the southern part of the Western Hemisphere coming together more closely while still retaining close links with the United States? The omens are not favourable, and much depends perhaps on the USA's ability to come to terms with what is a potentially revolutionary situation in most Latin American countries produced less by organized Communism as by the appalling gap between a small rich dominant minority and the totally illiterate and very miserable poor. But it is at any rate possible that the South American states may gradually draw closer together and form some economic union that makes sense, thus facilitating the industrialization which in spite of everything is making headway in all the countries concerned, and notably in Mexico and Brazil.

Once, however, the basic social problem has been tackled in many of the South American states where it is now acute; once industrialization has really got beyond the 'take-off' stage (as it seems to have done already in Mexico); then it may well be that the ties of language and of Latinity will become increasingly strong and that some kind of central institutions will be possible. If they are, it may well be as the result of the successful formation of a Western European entity. There is little doubt that South Americans would wish to diminish what they regard, rightly or wrongly, as too great dependence on the USA and that they might seek to emulate Europe, though not, it is sincerely to be hoped, a nationalist or Gaullist Europe.

The Middle East has, of course, the Arab League which now includes the non-Arab North African states of Morocco, Algeria, Tunisia, Libya, the Sudan and Egypt. The League is held together by a common language and culture, a common religion and by a hatred of Israel. It is divided, and rendered so far almost impotent by internal rivalries and by what is almost a war between two of its largest members. Nevertheless it exists and at least has the makings of an eventual Region. It is remarkable how the ancient religions have retained their hold over large areas in spite of the disruptive influence of nationalism. Though the immediate effect of the partial withdrawal of Great Power influence in the Middle East has undoubtedly exacerbated this nationalism, and though total withdrawal might admittedly intensify it still further for the time being, there is nevertheless a desire for unity based largely on Islam. In the comparatively recent past the idea of a Caliph was still extant. It is most improbable that this conception would be generally resurrected by 1984, but it is not impossible. No doubt it is going too far to suggest that the group might even within twenty years become a kind of confederation; but it is not impossible that by then it could be represented, by agreement, by one man in some new World Council. Israel ought, in principle, to join this bloc. You may say to believe in that is to believe in miracles. Perhaps. But it is not clear how this long-term political problem is to be solved peacefully under any alternative world political conception. Persia, too, might eventually be included in the group in spite of a different language and a schismatic religion. Otherwise she might be associated with the India grouping.

South-East Asia, it is true, presents fewer features of any future political group. At one stage in history Siam and what are now Cambodia, Laos and Vietnam were in some kind of association with China. This may happen again depending, no doubt, on the course of events in China itself. Alternatively the whole of this area might in some way be neutralized in a way satisfactory to China, India and the USA. Burma has had from time to time a close association with India and may have one in the future. The phrase 'Maphilindo' has already been coined to represent a vague federation of 150 million Malays (Malaysia, the Philippines and Indonesia). The possible future political alignment of this great region may even at this point be dimly discerned. Part may be associated with China, part with India, and part (with luck) with Oceania or the Western world.

Only Africa south of the Sahara may seem at present to be quite outside the realm of a Region even in the most optimistic imagining. The countries composing this enormous, though under-populated area, have, it is true, something in common. There is a common 'negritude' a dislike of the old colonial past, a fear of neo-colonialism and a universal detestation of apartheid. On the other hand there is no common language; complete incomprehension between the Africans of British and of French formation; much rivalry even between some of the English-speaking units; an early experience of failure (as in East Africa) of experiments in local federations. Above all, there is the fact that the great majority of the new nations concerned are really colonial artifacts, not based, for the most part, on any ancient national tradition, and therefore compelled, if they are not to disintegrate into their component tribes (as has already largely happened in the Congo), to cultivate an almost ferocious national particularism.

There remains one very large and important question mark – Japan. At the moment Japan is torn between the pull of America (which is likely for some time to remain the more powerful) and the pull of a new China. The attempt to colonize China and to assert a national will in East Asia regardless of American interests led to disaster in 1945. Since then Japan has had no policy, but she will clearly have to have one before another twenty years are up. If we are to assume that by then the United States has abandoned any attempt to influence events in South-East Asia and this region has been largely taken over by China, then indeed it would appear that Japan would have no choice save to make her peace with her great neighbour. But on the assumption that some kind of neutralization is possible in South-East Asia it is a fair guess that Japan will arrange some system whereby she is much closer to China than she is now while preserving special links with America. In any case the country will probably in twenty years' time have a population of at least 125 million and would probably qualify for a vote of its own in any future World Council.

No Regional scheme for world order can indeed be based purely on Regions. There must be great flexibility and one of the main postulates is that the various Regions will be able to strike some kind of balance, and thus be able happily to coexist. Nevertheless one may be in a more intimate relationship with another than with a third. On the whole it looks as if, always supposing that a new Europe emerges, enduring ties will be created between the latter and the African states south of the Sahara, perhaps also with the Middle East, and very likely (through the British connection) with the Indian complex. For their part the Americans, if they can come to terms with the new emergent forces in Latin America, should have special ties with that area, with 'Maphilindo' and no doubt also with Japan, which, however, could certainly not neglect her relationship with the China of the future. The Soviet Union, under such a scheme, might well continue to have 'special relations' with Eastern Europe and perhaps also with parts of the Middle East and even with India. In this way it might be hoped that the entire world would become increasingly interdependent and that some central machine would then be devised – and possibly situated in Europe – for ironing out differences arising between eight or nine major political complexes, and this might eventually become the organic centre of a real World Authority. But no doubt first there will have to be a struggle between China and Russia about who is to dominate the Eastern extremity of the USSR. Even if by 1984 there were only five or six genuine super-powers, the other regions might at least have got to the stage where they might, by agreement, be represented by one of their members in some reformed Security Council of nine or ten members. Would there then be any need for a World Assembly? Probably not; since if this great majority of nation-states were no longer completely independent, but rather part of a larger group, they would look for a settlement of their difficulties primarily in a regional context.

It is true that before such a situation can arise there may be a terrible period in which there may be only three, four or five 'poles of authority' struggling between themselves to exert their power over various areas in which no indigenous authority has so far emerged. The prophet George Orwell imagined (in 1945) the existence in 1984 of an 'Oceania' (North and South America, Britain, Australasia and South Africa), 'Eurasia' (which was really General de Gaulle's idea of '*L'Europe de l'Atlantique à l'Oural*') and 'Eastasia' (China, Japan and part of Siberia) all engaged in ferocious though non-nuclear wars designed (in theory) to extend the power of the one bloc or the other over the uncommitted area of Africa and South Asia, but (in practice) to maintain in power identical régimes of soul-less and co-opted bureaucrats. This nightmare remains a cautionary tale. It cannot be denied that the emergence of Regions, which now seems to be taking place before our very eyes, and whether we like it or not, may well result in some such situation as predicted by Orwell. But clearly the best way to prevent the fulfilment of this bleak prophecy would be to avoid a dangerous confrontation between what might be considered to be an American and a Russian Empire by a revival of the collectivity which in this book I have designated by its archaic name of Christendom, namely, that section of Europe which was part of the Roman Empire or Christianized from the West. Only by so doing, as it seems to me, can we advance towards a world balance and a real lowering of excessive tension.

In an age when man appears to be about to set foot on the moon; when armaments have reached such a pitch that they cannot possibly be used; when the world is already one from the point of view of communications and, in many respects, from that of human requirements, tastes and ordinary preferences; when the old ideologies are all wearing thin and the old barriers and incomprehensions are tending to dissolve under the increasing sum of ordinary human contacts, is it too much to hope that the human race may escape extinction by choosing the comparatively simple, and on the face of it, rational way towards salvation that Regionalism provides? The basic reason for this is that the new European experiment, if it succeeds, will be catching. Once the independent nation-state has been mastered and as it were tamed in one great region of the world, so it may be tamed in others. It is perfectly true that the absence of any common philosophy that is to say the absence of any common interpretation of the great principles such as democracy, liberty, human rights, and so on forbids the construction of any World State at the present time, and possibly not for many years. But that does not necessarily prevent the establishment of some Authority which would, basically, conform to general economic and political interests.

At the risk therefore of re-introducing King Charles' head, may I repeat that the chances of starting some move in this general direction are largely conditioned by what happens in the old home of the Industrial Revolution, the cradle of the Western World, namely, Europe. If one can here adopt a regional system whereby certain decisions, even in the sphere of foreign policy and defence, are taken in common – and one will be very close to that when and if Britain joins the EEC – then the successful development of such a system might well set a tremendous example. It is, however, useless to think that a *Europe des Etats* would do anything save encourage nationalism in all the emergent countries. *Fiat gloria, ruat coelum.* The old stale ideologies, the confrontations, the manifest destinies of 130 nation-states will all persist. Eventually of course there will be a war. Is our civilization really doomed to perish in this stupid and miserable way? Not if the younger generation in all our ancient lands oblige their governments to take the first essential step namely, the real unification of a democratic Europe.

CHAPTER ELEVEN

*

General Conclusion

THIS book has probably established one thing. If the Community which has now been set up in Western Europe is to continue, if it is going to be a hopeful experiment favouring world peace, if it is to enable its component parts, namely, the ancient nation-states of Europe to fulfil their real destiny and not to lapse gradually into sheer provincialism or satellization, it must possess certain supra-national powers. It can have no such powers, and it will therefore fairly soon join the limbo of fine projects and frustrated hopes, unless the present suspicious and chauvinistic mood of France changes and unless both she and Britain can come together in accordance with a genuine economic and political supra-national plan. Economically therefore Britain should announce her intention of joining the EEC without previous conditions save for agreement on a suitable voting formula, the consent of EFTA, and some important bargain struck about the nature of the transitional régime that would be applied to her and her associates and a handful of hard-core problems. Politically she should say that what she wants is that a common defence and foreign policy will be aimed at in a Council of Ministers in which there will be no hegemony, but rather a determination to arrive at joint decisions with the aid of an independent political commission and a resolve to take decisions in certain limited spheres by a qualified majority vote. All this should be agreed in advance together with the grant, in principle, of greater powers to the existing Parliament of Europe.

One would have thought that any government in this country worthy of its salt, irrespective of party, would see the immense advantage of pursuing such a policy (for long recommended by my own organization, known as 'Britain in Europe', whose policy statement of April 1963 is quoted in Appendix 2) and thus directly appealing to all the best, and incidentally all the pro-British elements on the continent of Europe. The danger is that Her Majesty's Government, whether Tory or Labour, will do no such thing, but will rather toy with the idea of entering a Europe of nation-states on the lines recommended by General de Gaulle. It is quite true that it would be excellent to find some formula whereby the British and French nuclear forces could be co-ordinated, within the framework of the Western Alliance, in the interests of Europe as a whole. It is even more true that no solution for the problem of our relationship with the Continent can be found unless there is a genuine agreement between ourselves and France. It follows that Anglo-French co-operation on a basis of complete equality must be achieved before any lasting European unity can come into existence. But to think that a Western Europe which is at present in the process of rejecting French hegemony can come into existence on the basis of some Anglo-French, still less of some British, hegemony is a pure illusion. The other states of the EEC, and notably Germany, simply would not take it. Nor would it be likely to appeal to our present EFTA colleagues. We cannot, therefore, as it were, buy our way into the Common Market by trying to play up to the forces which want to disrupt it politically; we can only, if we really wish to enjoy the benefits of economic unity, go the whole political hog and seek, in so doing, to give a lead to the new Community which is still struggling to form itself on the other side of the Channel.

Let no one think that such a move on our part would be breaking with our historic past. On the contrary, it is only by demonstrating that a modern Britain is in favour, not of an outworn and narrow nationalism, but rather of a genuine international democracy of a new type, that we can advance towards a happier destiny. There is at present a wealth of frustrated idealism in Britain which wants to be harnessed to some great cause. The Commonwealth, valuable as it is, is increasingly seen to be something that, in the very nature of things, cannot absorb the energies of the ex-metropolis, which would, it seems, be guilty of neo-colonialism if it tried to impose itself on its ex-Empire overmuch. If this creative urge is not going to go sour on us, as it may go sour in Germany also (and we know what that can mean), it simply must be given a definite and unquestioned goal. What could this be other than a United Europe? How otherwise can the young men and women of Britain feel that they are pulling their weight and no longer be exclusively concerned with their own immediate affairs in total disregard of the revolutionary world around them?

One thing, however, does stand out from this brief examination of the European Idea. It is that the difficulties in the way of putting it into full operation are still enormous and that great imagination and leadership will be necessary if it is to prevail. It is not only that the force of inertia tells against the adoption of any far-reaching reforms affecting the power of the nation-state; it is also because the nation-state is still very much concerned to preserve itself in all its ancient, separate sufficiency. Against this, and in favour of Europe, are the pressures of the modern world, the demands of industry, the contradictions invoked in the age of the hydrogen bomb, by the spirit of nationalism itself, the impasse of the free society subjected in the nature of things to many controls. We must hope that these last forces will triumph and, if we can, we must give them a helping hand. To start off right is the thing; and once we do start off right the tide of history itself may well lead us to the desired destination.

There is another lion in the path, which has to be looked squarely in the eye. I have tried to show that in the continuance, the development and the enlargement of the present EEC lies the only hope for European unity. If it collapses, there is only the grim prospect of an exacerbated and provincial nationalism and a lower standard of living, or of a merger of Europe's ancient nations with one super-state or the other. Yet the EEC contains one ancient nation which is divided. Can it continue for long in this condition, or will the nationalist forces in Germany prove too strong and result in some reunification on terms not consonant with the continued existence of the EEC?

All we can say is that the forces binding the greater part of Germany, namely, the Federal Republic, to the West, would be greatly strengthened if Britain were able to join the Community. For then it would be possible to show that the bulk of the Germans were part of something which could stand on its own feet, as the 'Union' of Germany and France clearly cannot, based as it must be, if it is to endure, on the hegemony of only one partner, and quite incapable of assuming by itself the defence of the whole Community. In a Community including Britain the Germans would feel that they had an equal part to play together with their great partners, they would thus have a sense of responsibility and a sense of purpose. The feeling that the East was something which must be 'recovered' in the immediate future would lose its intensity. It would be replaced by a feeling that the example of a unified West in which Germany was playing a leading part was so impressive that in due course, and by the nature of things, the Soviet Union would be obliged to loosen its grip and agree to some arrangement whereby Eastern Germany and other Eastern European states were in some way associated with a Western Europe sufficiently strong to agree to the departure of American troops, just as Soviet troops would be evacuated to Russia. Besides, if Britain comes in, no hegemony will be possible, if for no other reason than that neither the British nor the French would accept any such system, and consequently a real Community which will also absorb Germany and Italy as equals, will be formed as the only possible solution.

There is no denying that the problem of the reunification of the Germans is one that cannot be shelved or pushed under the rug when it comes to considering the future of the EEC. From the German point of view it must colour their judgment as to the desirability or otherwise of Britain joining the Community. One thing is certain: the Germans do not wish the American troops to return to America even if, by so doing, they might make a negotiation with the USSR possible. On the other hand, judging from Franz Josef Strauss' recent rather brilliant book, *The Grand Design*, they seem to feel that it is only if a Western Europe is formed in a political sense, including Britain, that there is any question of rising above the division of Germany, and consequently of Europe, and the perpetuation of the so-called status quo. What they might realize, perhaps, is that though this is true enough, their actual and prospective European partners are just not prepared to take grave risks to achieve the reunification of the Germans or even to insist, as Herr Strauss would wish, on the right of the Germans to go and settle anywhere in Europe where their forebears have lived previously. The way to achieve legitimate German ends, surely, is for the Germans first to join a community in which they really do feel and are, at least the equals of Britain and France, and then, when the new machine had got run in, to make it plain that it is no longer a question of restoring the Fatherland, but simply of entering, as a new group, into closer relationship with, not only the Eastern Germans, but also the non-Soviet nations of Eastern Europe.

The day of the all-German settlement is therefore doubtless still far distant, but, short of communization, it can only be imagined at all if the greater part of Europe first comes together in a physical sense, that is to say produces some real union which is not based on the hegemony of any one power, but on genuinely European institutions. For otherwise the two giants, however much they may wish to live at peace, will be condemned to an eternal and fruitless 'confrontation', neither side being able to retire without feeling that his cause is lost if he does so, and Germany remaining permanently divided. Only if an autonomous Europe is formed, too weak (by comparison with the giants) to be aggressive, too strong to be overawed, is any peaceful union at all conceivable. And even then for a long time one part will probably be in closer touch with the West and one with the East. We must indeed hope that this prospect will gradually recommend itself to all the peoples of the West. But first Britain must join the Common Market. If she does so she will, admittedly, be entering into close association with a vigorous and rather unpredictable Germany. But there is absolutely no doubt that the energies of this dynamic and sundered nation may be devoted to much more undesirable ends if they are not treated as an absolute equal by their immediate Western European neighbours.

For Britain to join there must be to some extent a change of heart in France. But there must also be a complete change of heart in Britain. No longer must it be imagined by the bulk of the British that joining the EEC is simply a device for enabling our products to enjoy a wider home market and nothing else. We must realize that what is involved is the creation of a new form of political union in which we would certainly play a leading part, but in which also we should only be part of a larger whole. For both the British and the French, who are, of all the Europeans, the ones with the longest national tradition, acceptance of this thesis is the hardest thing of all. And yet it must be accepted if either nation is going to endure in the sense of playing a really significant part in our modern civilization. It is literally true of us that if we would find ourselves we must first lose ourselves. The old rivals, the old friend-enemies, must first come freely together if Feranghistan is ever to be formed as a durable whole.

It also appears from our study, I think, that far and away the best way of producing this union, and the best adapted to our modern world, is for us all to apply what are called 'Community technique's in the political and in the economic field. This seems to be a technique admirably suited for nation-states which are ready to come together in something which is more than a mere alliance, or even than an old-fashioned confederation, but nevertheless much less all-embracing than an actual super-state. For this to happen, there is no need, to start off with, for a common European 'patriotism'. This would not emerge for a considerable number of years. It would be long before an Englishman or a Frenchman, when asked what his nationality was, would reply 'I am a European', in the same way as a man from California says naturally 'I am an American'. But what would be necessary from the start would be a sense of purpose and a conviction that, if one belonged in the first instance to one's native land, one belonged in the second instance to Europe.

It might be that the mass of people in the countries concerned would not even get as far as this for many years (though much would depend on the way in which the idea was presented in the schools), but it would have to be from the start the conviction of the 'ruling few', of the greater part of the intellectuals, of the civil servants who for the most part would be working the machinery of the Community. Only if they were so convinced would it be possible for the Commission to stand up to the pressures of the nation-state which would continue to be exercised in the Council of Ministers. Only if the Ministers – the representatives of the peoples – were themselves convinced would it be possible for themselves to stand up to similar pressures. It is obvious that a man like Robert Schuman would be more inclined to find a common way than a man like, shall we say, Franz Josef Strauss. It is also quite arguable, that if the external presures are largely removed, the Strausses will be more numerous than the Schumans.

This indeed is the crucial point. In international affairs men are unfortunately more often actuated by fear than by considerations of their own or their neighbours' good. The European Idea came to fruition between 1951 and 1957 largely owing to the operation of fear, fear of the Russians, even some suspicions of the Americans, certainly fear of a relapse into that continental anarchy which had only recently produced such indescribably frightful results. All these fears have worn off. All Europe has become much richer in the last fifteen years. Russia has quarrelled with China. The loss of empires has had no markedly impoverishing effect. Why should we do difficult and perhaps dangerous things in the belief, which may perhaps not be justified, that we should all be much better off if we created a new Community in Western Europe? Why not just carry on as we are and hope for the best? 'Death is the end of life: ah, why should life all labour be?'

It is possible that such arguments may become increasingly powerful as the years go by. They may prevent our joining the Common Market owing to a sheer lack of will to overcome the obstacles still in the way. They may even prevent the Six themselves from taking the *saltus mortalis* into the third phase of the Treaty. Even an economic recession of some magnitude might not necessarily help: for whereas it might well demonstrate the urgent necessity of achieving an economic union of all Europe, it might also make it all the more difficult for governments to take the immediately unpleasant measures to achieve this, such as allowing more competition from abroad when many of their own fellow-citizens are out of work. All this, provided the reader has been convinced by my general analysis, is really an argument in favour of going ahead as fast as we can and, in default of an actual chance of joining the Community, at least of making our own attitude and our policy entirely clear.

What, then, should any British government do? Well, there is one thing that it could and should do, and that is to explain to the British people what the long-term objective really is. *Not* neutralism: *not* carrying on alone with the Commonwealth and a diminishing EFTA: *not* union with America: but rather a new form of association with our European neighbours within the Western Alliance which would preserve our ancient institutions of our age-long way of life. Vague assurances that we are in favour of 'Europe'; that we want in principle to be part of a larger market: that we also want to be 'Europeans' and at the same time make an 'independent contribution to peace-keeping in the Indian Ocean'; that we feel that the best thing would be for the Six to join EFTA; that, though European, we must preserve an independent foreign policy; all these are entirely beside the point. The question is do we, or do we not, still want to sign the Treaty of Rome establishing the EEC; do we, or do we not, want to join some Political and Defence Community of the type outlined above; are we prepared to undertake the obligations clearly inherent in all these things; and above all are we prepared to come out and say so?

Nations, after all, cannot exist without some idea of what their right place is in the world and what they hope that the next generation may be able to accomplish. All human endeavour has its tragic side. No political end is ever wholly achieved, and when it is partially achieved there is always some other objective stretching away beyond. But in Europe at any rate there is no doubt that the national idea, the idea that the inhabitants of any one country have only one overriding duty, namely, to push the interests of their particular state, though it may be strong enough to frustrate the victory of any alternative ideology, has probably had its day. We may not any longer believe in the inevitability of progress – who could, with the dreadful example of man's inherent ferocity all around us? – but at least we can have before us some limited, concrete and on the face of it realizable end which might, as we see it also contribute to the general good of humanity. Convinced Communists no doubt have this objective also; but it is for us to see that it can be achieved without the appalling loss of individual liberty which Communism demands.

Mr Gaitskell said three years ago, in a moment of passion, that a thousand years of history should prevent us from associating ourselves, in any real political sense, with the EEC. It is always possible to appeal to history in support of any preconceived idea. His was undoubtedly that there was a sort of unsurmountable ideological gulf between us and our continental neighbours that would prevent us from ever joining them in a physical sense. Rather, we should, it seemed, with the Commonwealth, seek to maintain an independent rôle in the world and endeavour to carry on in some new form the old traditions of the Empire. I suggest that precisely the contrary is true. As I hope I have shown, a thousand years of history prove exactly the reverse, namely that the centre and origin of the civilization that has now spread over the globe should at long last form the fruit for which it was evidently the flower and that only by helping to do this can we, so far as Britain is concerned, preserve something of the great heritage which our ancestors have

137

left us, which we can now further develop provided we have the imagination and the will.

It may be that some of the details of the scheme which I personally favour are faulty. It is possible to think of other ways in which the European Idea could be put into practical execution. There is room, within the general conception, for all sorts of plans. But what is certain is that some project for combining the talents of all the great nations of Europe is now a burning political necessity. The extraordinary brilliance of the great French administrators, the high intelligence and resourcefulness of the Italians, the organizing power of the Germans, the diligence and honesty of the Dutch, the shrewd business-sense of the Belgians, the democratic idealism of the Scandinavians, the wisdom and practical sense of the British, yes, even eventually the dour obstinacy and pride of Spain, all are required to form the new Community which, in free association with North America, might transform the world political scene and bring about a peace in which from Montana to Sinkiang the missiles could gradually moulder in their silos, the emergent nations no longer fear Imperialism nor the West Communism, but all combine to promote the general welfare of mankind.

If this is a dream, it is a worthwhile dream. If anything is worth struggling for, it is this. We should not be put off by the slowness of progress. Certainly we shall not, as a nation, be down and out if we cannot get into the Market in the fairly near future. Provided there is no failure of the national will, we shall of course make the best of the alternatives to joining. Perhaps an economic crisis might even stimulate this national will. But that we and other European nations will still be in a dangerous situation if the dream really fades and we have to make do with one of these alternatives no one can possibly doubt. If in this country we can all, or most of us, say that a European solution on the broad lines that I have ventured to describe is what we want then, in spite of the difficulties, we shall have gone a long way towards achieving it. First the will, then the concept, then the act.

APPENDIX 1

*

Declaration by Common Market Campaign, May 1961

BRITAIN must decide, and decide soon, whether she is prepared to play her full part in the dynamic new power which has arisen in Europe, or whether she is to be increasingly cut off from the Continent, both politically and economically. Equally the Six must soon decide whether they are prepared to facilitate the entry of the United Kingdom into the Common Market or whether they prefer to run the very real risks involved in a continued political division of Western Europe.

Repeated attempts by the United Kingdom to secure economic participation without accepting political responsibilities have failed. Now what is required is a clear statement that we are ready to assume our responsibilities in Europe. This means accepting the basic principles of the Rome Treaty, including a Common Tariff, while negotiating an agreement to meet the special needs of Britain, the Commonwealth and the European Free Trade Association. The process will necessarily involve limiting our complete freedom of action in the economic field, as we have already done in the military.

No one can doubt the force and momentum of the European Economic Community. Its policy is proving more liberal, both politically and economically, than originally seemed likely, which makes it easier for Britain to join. If we are to prevent a dangerous split in Europe, time is short, and not on our side. To count on some eventual collapse of the European Economic Community would be most unwise.

Three main, admittedly difficult, problems have to be solved

139

before we can be associated with the Community of the Six. They are our special economic relationship with the Commonwealth, our system of agricultural supports, and our relationship with our partners in the European Free Trade Association, especially those who are politically neutral. All these problems could, we believe, be solved in negotiations. But negotiations will only be possible if we first declare our willingness, subject to their successful outcome, to join the European Economic Community – a Community in which no one nation will ultimately have the power of veto.

Unless we make this attempt, Europe, already split by the Iron Curtain, will be still further divided; for her part, Britain will be in increasing danger of becoming a backwater, both politically and economically. If, however, the negotiations succeed, we shall become part of a new dynamic power, to the benefit of all branches of our economy, of our sister nations in the Commonwealth, of our European Free Trade Association partners, and indeed of the present members of the European Economic Community.

We therefore believe that Her Majesty's Government, after the necessary consultation with the Commonwealth and the European Free Trade Association, should formally and explicitly declare their readiness in principle to join the European Economic Community and to accept the institutions of the Treaty of Rome. Only thus can the Commonwealth, of which the United Kingdom would remain the senior partner, be associated with a vast, new, outward-looking political organization, capable of accumulating and deploying the necessary capital for the development of the less fortunate nations of the world. And only so can Britain ensure for herself the place which is her due in the Atlantic Community of the future.

In expressing this conviction it is the wish of the undersigned, who are drawn from all three political parties, or from none, and who represent many differing fields of activity, to give the Government the assurance that if they decide to act as suggested they will enjoy widespread and influential support in the Nation.

APPENDIX 2

*

Policy Statement Issued by 'Britain in Europe',
March 1963

BRITAIN in Europe, now incorporating the Common Market Campaign, stands for the entry of the United Kingdom into a European Economic and Political Community. The broad economic terms for entry should, in its view, be those which seemed to be attainable during the later stages of the Brussels negotiations. On the political side, Britain in Europe stands for Britain's participation in a European ministerial political and defence Council so designed as to produce effective action within the framework of the Western Alliance; and independent political commission to advise this Council and to represent a European as opposed to purely national views; and greater powers for the existing European Parliament. Britain in Europe will represent the case for our joining Europe on these economic and political conditions thus preparing for the day when negotiations for an outward looking community may be resumed and successfully concluded.

APPENDIX 3

*

Correspondence with Count Richard Coudenhove-Kalergi

Letter from Lord Gladwyn to Count Coudenhove-Kalergi, 27 July 1965:

I READ in Le Monde of July 25th that the French Committee of the Paneuropean Union has stated in its last monthly bulletin that attempts to 'force the hand of France' have 'resulted in a fresh check to the movement towards European Union'; that 'Professor Hallstein's mistake' was 'a demonstration of the inefficacy of supranational power'; and that 'reconciliation of opposing interests cannot be achieved by majority voting', but only by a 'process of mutual persuasion and a spirit of compromise'.

The only basis for a Europe which is more than a collection of totally independent nations is the Treaty of Rome. This contains clear provision for majority voting at a certain date, in other words for a limited, but definite measure of 'supranational power'. It is unquestionable that France freely signed this Treaty and that she is consequently bound by it. It follows that the thesis of your French Committee cannot be accepted by anyone who believes in the construction of Europe still less by anyone who still believes in the sanctity of treaties and the Rule of Law. Unless, therefore, this thesis is repudiated by the Paneuropean Union, I must request you to remove my name from the list of members of your Comité d'Honneur.

Letter from Count Coudenhove-Kalergi to Lord Gladwyn, 3 August 1965:

The Paneuropean Union is, since 1924, a democratic organization. Therefore her national groups must be free to express their respective views, whether I share or not. Personally, I am fed up with the quarrel about who is responsible for the present most regrettable crisis. The only thing that interests me is how to go ahead on the stony road leading to a United States of Europe. Many of my friends believe that this is possible only against the Fifth Republic. I am convinced of the contrary: Europe cannot be separated from France, nor France from de Gaulle.

Whatever you now decide to do, I thank you for your splendid campaign for a United Europe including Great Britain.

Extracts from a letter from Monsieur Terrenoire to Count Coudenhove-Kalergi:

Mr Terrenoire is 'surprised by the excessively contentious tone of the letter of the ex-Ambassador to France and even more astonished that he should urge France to respect a Treaty which his own country contested for so long before becoming interested in it. Perhaps therefore it is only a question of a misunderstanding. Lord Gladwyn, indeed, confuses decisions which the Council of Ministers has to take without the application of the unanimity rule and the progressive realization of supra-national power by the Commission at present presided over by Professor Hallstein. Does Lord Gladwyn accept the idea of one day confiding the destiny of Britain to a body totally independent of the Crown and of the House of Commons? I venture to doubt it. As for majority voting in the Council of Members of the EEC all those who believe in the harmonious construction of Europe should hope that, in a general way, it will be applied with prudence and discretion, but more particularly "in all circumstances where major national responsibilities would be at stake". This is what we wrote in our Bulletin and we persist in believing that mutual persuasion and a spirit of compromise will always be more constructive and less risky than any mechanical counting of heads.'

Letter from Lord Gladwyn to Count Coudenhove-Kalergi, 24 August 1965:

Many thanks for your letter of 3rd August. I have now seen extracts from the letter addressed to you on this subject by Monsieur Louis Terrenoire.

Let me say at once that it is *not* a question of making Europe 'against the Fifth Republic'. This would not only be highly undesirable, but, as I see it, impossible. Europe cannot be constructed without France, though I believe myself that it cannot be constructed without Britain either. Since I left Paris it has been my chief concern to establish this essential fact. Nobody could be more conscious of the necessity of Franco-British co-operation than I am. Nobody could be more appreciative of, and welcome more warmly, the great French national 'redressement' which has transformed the country during the last seven years. Nobody, finally, has tried harder than I have to persuade my compatriots that it was essential for this country to join France in the EEC on a footing of complete equality and to accept in advance all the obligations and political implications of the Treaty of Rome. And what do I now discover? If the French Committee of the Paneuropean Movement is to be believed, it is France herself which is not prepared to accept these obligations!

What is tragic is that the obligations and implications in question were specifically accepted by Mr Edward Heath speaking in the name of the British Government on 14th April, 1962. There is little doubt that, had the negotiations not been broken off by France, the British nation would have willingly followed this governmental lead. How Monsieur Terrenoire can say that we 'contested' this Treaty is therefore hard to understand. It cannot be disputed that we accepted the Treaty as it stands, without any amendments. What was being negotiated was essentially conditions of a transitional character designed to cushion the shock to our economy and that of certain other countries, of an immediate reversal of our present agricultural policy. This Treaty which we were prepared to accept provides, as we all know, in Article 148 for qualified majority voting, under which even a Great Power can, in the last resort, and in certain limited circumstances be overruled on a matter which it may even deem to be contrary to its vital interests. The Treaty also contains the most specific provisions in Articles 155–163 for what can only be described as a 'supra-national' rôle for the independent Commission which (as the Treaty says) 'disposes of a power of decision of its own'. It is unquestionable that if we had accepted these obligations by signing the Treaty – as Mr Heath announced we would – we would not have subsequently repudiated it. More and more the conviction in this country is growing that we ought to sign the Treaty if we are allowed to do so. And if we do sign the Treaty we shall do our best to see that it is properly carried out by all parties.

In its paper entitled 'The Crisis of the Common Market' the French Committee of the Paneuropean Union after a long complaint about French difficulty in getting their partners to give them satisfaction on agriculture – a struggle which nevertheless admittedly resulted in a 'French victory' – maintains that the Commission should not have submitted a scheme for the financing of the agreed common agricultural policy which allotted to itself any rôle of 'arbiter'. The actual proposals submitted by the Commission for the approval of a common budget were put forward only as a basis for discussion, and even if they are deemed to be 'premature' or even 'tactless', there is no doubt that some such scheme will have eventually to be approved if there is to be any form of common budget and if the Assembly is to play any rôle at all. In no case can it legitimately be said that the Commission was violating in any way either the letter, still less the spirit of the Treaty.

What therefore I found especially disturbing in the paper of the French Committee was the flat statement that 'Professor Hallstein's error' had 'demonstrated the ineffectiveness of a supra-national power'; that the reconciliation of opposing theses or interests cannot be effected by majority decisions, more especially if it is a question of 'major national responsibilities'; and that such a reconciliation can only be the result of 'reciprocal persuasion and a spirit of compromise'. Nobody denies that in practice the intelligent system devised by the authors of the Treaty of Rome will normally result in decisions being reached by a 'process of persuasion'. But the point is that if the ultimate sanction is repudiated in advance by any one signatory the process of persuasion cannot even begin, and the Community is reduced to a collection of totally independent sovereign nation-states which is of course a state of affairs exactly opposite to that postulated by the Treaty. It is in my view lamentable that France should have apparently placed herself in an untenable position, and we can only hope that she will not persist in this mistaken course.

It is all the more regrettable since already sincere and friendly voices are being heard advocating an 'Atlantic' Customs Union to which at any rate Britain might adhere. Rebuffed by her nearest, and in principle our dearest neighbour, who in any case now shows signs of not wanting to form any real European Union, the temptation for us to accept such an invitation, if made, will obviously be great. If we cannot construct the European 'pillar' and form a valid alliance with America on this basis, what is there for us to do but encourage the Americans to form some kind of 'Anglo-Saxon' federation, though it may be, of course that the Germans and the Italians, despairing of 'Europe' might be attracted by it too. Is this really what France would desire? I cannot believe it.

Nevertheless, the sands are now running out. The chances of Britain joining Europe and consequently of joining a France conscious of her responsibilities are still open, but not, I feel, for very long. Together we could, with our other European friends, achieve wonders. But not if we remain divided. Must the whole notion of a supra-national European body (which is the only means whereby we could come together) really disappear? If you yourself no longer favour this last conception, then I must certainly resign from your Comité d'Honneur. But if you do then you certainly cannot logically share the opinions of your French Committee.

[*I subsequently did resign.*]

APPENDIX 4

*

Extracts from Speech Delivered by Lord Gladwyn at the Liberal Party Assembly at Scarborough on 23 September 1965:

IN the latest of his 'Press Conferences' General de Gaulle has more or less ordered his European partners to revise the Treaty of Rome, which, as you all know, specially provides in Article 155 for certain well-defined 'powers of decision' to be conferred on the Brussels Commission and for qualified majority voting in the Council of Ministers at the beginning of the so-called 'Third Stage' on 1 January 1966. Both these provisions he now rejects, apparently for the reasons that they will limit the entire freedom of action of France and were concluded before he came into power. The Treaty of Rome was, however, formally ratified by the French Parliament only eight years ago. We can hardly suppose that if the General is unsuccessful in inducing the co-signatories of the Treaty to revise it in a sense which would deprive it of all real content, he will actually denounce it unilaterally; but he would no doubt do his best in that event to see that the system does not operate as intended, at any rate for so long as he is in command. The danger is that the Five, confronted with this non-co-operation, will agree to revise or modify the Treaty in the sense desired by the General, thereby rendering it completely ineffective.

What could therefore have a tremendous effect in Europe would be if we could only persuade our Government to say definitely (*a*) that it is still their firm intention to sign the Treaty of Rome as soon as they are permitted to do so, and (*b*) that for their part they regard the Treaty as the right basis for the kind of Europe which we should hope to join.

Negotiations for our entry, when resumed, should – they ought to announce – apart from necessary adjustments such as the Voting Formula, be restricted to interim arrangements necessary to adapt our economy and those of EFTA and the Commonwealth members affected to the new system which will operate in Western Europe once the EEC, extended so as to include ourselves and the other candidates, is allowed to progress in accordance with the Treaty.

But more than that. The Government should also announce that it is firmly wedded to the general idea of a meaningful European Community in the political and defence spheres as well. Not a Federation – that is a rather old-fashioned, eighteenth-century conception which can hardly apply to the modern nation-states of Europe – but rather a Political and Defence Community which will function on new and modern lines, notably by applying the techniques which, until repudiated by General de Gaulle, were the pride and glory of the new European Idea, namely an Independent Commission and the principle of qualified majority voting in certain definite and limited spheres. . . .

Let no one be misled by siren voices maintaining that, thanks to the French President, we may now soon join a cosy 'Europe of States'. For it is no good thinking that such a system, which could only operate, if it operated at all, on an acknowledged Franco-British nuclear hegemony bearing no relation to NATO would be willingly accepted by the Germans, the Italians or the Dutch, who would clearly prefer a straight alliance, or even some economic union, with America. Nor would it even be consonant with the maintenance of a European customs union and common market, for that pre-supposes at least a minimum of political integration. And that very word is anathema to the old-fashioned and nationalistic mind. All that would happen if we were so misguided as to fall for this idea would be that

Europe would suffer the opposite of integration, namely dis-integration, either becoming a satrapy of the United States, or of the Soviet Union, or more probably remaining divided under the influence of both.

No, what this country would clearly go for if only it had a foreign policy, is the achievement in Western Europe of a genuinely supra-national Community with a common economic foreign and defence policy; this Community to be in association with the present neutrals and eventually perhaps even with certain Eastern European states; the whole constituting a valid partner of America in some revised 'Atlantic' system. . . .

Fellow delegates, we are informed in effect by the ruler of France that the British people will not accept any Community solution which transcends the bounds of the present nation-state. Who, I respectfully ask, is the ruler of France to tell us what we shall accept or not accept? In his own country he may hold up progress towards a real Community, though I believe that even there the necessity of creating Europe will prevail over an archaic nationalism, which in an age of Super Powers and Super Bombs, is about as relevant to our modern problems as the arquebus or the First Crusade. But for our part we can, if we will, declare to our friends in Europe, and indeed in France itself, that we stand for something very different, for a principle that may be of service not only to us in this small continent, but to all humanity. If France for the moment cannot or will not lead Europe in this direction let Britain, with all the zeal of a convert, take up the torch from her faltering fingers. And let this message go out from our united Assembly. Good Europeans should not lose heart. Hold out only a little longer and you will find Britain joining a free and democratic Europe with common institutions capable of producing common decisions, which, as Milton said of England, will, by its example, teach other nations how to live.

INDEX

Index

153

Index